Silent Tears I've Cried

By Shelly Knox

Printed in the United States of America.

Book Design and Formatted by Barnett Publishing

ISBN - Paperback: 979-8-9876636-9-1

Disclaimer

I have tried to recreate events, locales, and conversations from my memories of them. To maintain their anonymity in some instances I have changed the names of individuals and places. I may have changed some identifying characteristics and details, such as physical properties, occupations, and places of residence.

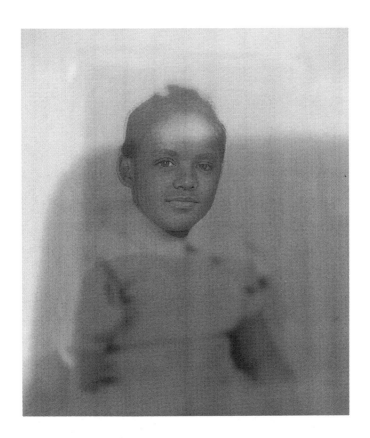

Silent Tears I've Cried by Shelly Knox

RESOURCES

- SUICIDE HOTLINE 800-273-8255
- WOAR (PHILADELPHIA CENTER AGAINST SEXUAL VIOLENCE) 215-985-3315
- 24-HOUR MENTAL HEALTH CRISIS: 800-662-4357

Dedication To

Victims of abuse,

To know you're not in this alone ...

We can fight this fight together.

"See the glory and don't know the story" Mikki Rogers

Table of Contents

Introduction

(By Shelly's fifth-grade Latin teacher)

"Only those of us who have walked on sharp stones can tell others what it is like. Shelly Knox, the author of this book, has been thrown down on such stones. She has known such a path all her fifty-four years.

In this life, no one gets a prize for those who suffered the most. There is no thick skin to cover the innocence of a child. The inward retreat of a constantly abused child knows almost no relief.

As I read this book, my caring heart feels her earliest wounds. I started teaching Latin to Shelly in fifth grade when she was nine years old. Her ebony skin shone. A child with nowhere to turn. There was no unconditional love, no safety for her from any family, but she did have a few friends, not many, from the neighborhood. That could help her out somewhat in her time of trouble.

Such an intolerable life does produce an extreme need for relief, even an exit strategy. As a child, Shelly began to look for ways to take her life.

military to help take care of the family as well. My parents, Saran, and Clifford met when they worked down on the waterfront. They dated for a while My *mother* became pregnant with me, and that's when they decided to get married. This pregnancy was unexpected, as was my mother's firstborn, but that's another story. They were already living in a duplex on 18th Street in Philadelphia.

While they were living there, I had no babysitter and my mother had to take me everywhere she went, any time of night or day. Before long, my father moved out and my cousin Rocco moved into the apartment upstairs. He then became my babysitter. He would occasionally look after me for hours, and occasionally even for days at a time. There were times when she left me alone with him and his company upstairs, and other times when he was alone. Sometimes, he would leave me alone downstairs in my crib while he watched me somehow from upstairs. There were times when his company made sure I ate and at other times, I didn't eat at all. I ate when he felt like feeding me or when he got tired of hearing me cry. Rocco really didn't care whether I ate or not. I often ate large pieces of sheetrock out of the wall, the thread out of the carpet, and whatever was on the floor or in my

Silent Tears I've Cried by Shelly Knox

diaper. I was hungry. I didn't know any better. It was like Saran didn't realize she had a hungry baby at home. I ate so much sheetrock, over time, it was this enormous hole in the wall. I became very sick because of all the lead I had eaten at home. Where was the motherly instinct? I was only 15 months old when she started leaving me this way, for days on end. I had no childhood, no idea how I was supposed to be, what life was supposed to be like.

Eventually, social services threatened to take me away if the lead wasn't removed from the home. While the work was being done at the home, I went to stay with my aunt, who was raising my brother at the time. Finally, the work was done, but it took some time. I had to have blood levels drawn from time to time, then eventually my blood levels went back normal. I went back to stay with my mom at this time. I was always being switched from house to house and school to school.

In general, my mother had no time for children and after she had me, she was constantly on the go, as if she had no kids at home. Saran was a gambler and an alcoholic. Whatever money she had gone to, poker games and the casino. She had many rough nights of gambling cards, which led to us never having food or clothes. She never had any money for anything else. My mother's life wasn't stable, and the funds weren't there at all, so her sister and her sister's husband, who were raising my brother, took me in as well. What a blessing. There wasn't anything my mother (aunt) wouldn't do for her brothers and sister, including raising her sister's children and helping her with her bills. My aunt sold my mother her home on 18th street for a very small price. Since she'd gotten married and started a family, my aunt was doing well for herself. She had money enough to live a comfortable life, so that was never an issue when we were with her.

Originally, (Mom) Saran had taken my brother down south at an early age and just left him there with other family members and didn't go back to get him. Our mother (aunt) went to get him and decided to raise him herself. She did so much for him, and she took good care of him as a mother would. He started calling her mom. Right now, to this day, he feels the same way.

Our aunt (I've always referred to her as Mom, too, as that is how I think of her) always made sure we didn't want for anything. We had the finest clothes, food in the freezer, and whatever else we needed

Silent Tears I've Cried by Shelly Knox

or wanted. We were very spoiled in that house on Napa Street.

Some cousins were jealous of us. We were raised by our aunt. How is she, our mother?

When I reached my teenage years, I began to realize I really did have everything I wanted and just about everything I needed, living with my aunt. But, most important of all, I realized if you don't have love; you don't have anything. The only bad thing was, when I was home, I would always get beatings with one or two extension cords or belts. I deserved them and other times I didn't.

Later, when my aunt and uncle retired, they continued to keep us in their home, to make sure that we both were taken care of. Both were nice quiet individuals. They drank too, but not as heavy as my parents and other relatives. They would do anything for a person, especially for my mother. Even though my aunt Elsa was married, she still had her boyfriends on the side. Uncle Tom didn't care whether she was home. Once he retired, he mostly stayed home and didn't go to many places. There were many times when I was left home with him, and other times I was at various house parties with the family, though sometimes they would get a babysitter.

If I ever acted up, it would be time to send me right to my mother's. I don't care what my brother did. He never went back to my mom's to stay.

I had a lot of friends at my aunt's (mom) I could go out and play every day. When I was 18th, I didn't have friends in the neighborhood. From time to time, I'd go outside and play in the playground or in front of the door, but not that often.

My mom (aunt) always kept me in nice pretty dresses. Every time you saw me, I had on whatever clothes my aunt (mom) bought for me.

My parents were always fussing and fighting. Even though they seemed to always be hanging out, partying, and having a good time, as if they had no responsibilities at home, they weren't always hanging out together. My mother didn't mind going out with or without her husband, nor did she care who was the babysitter. She'd always find someone, whether it be a man, woman, boy, girl, my cousins, or whoever. Sometimes, she'd just take me with her, no matter how late it was. This would take place every week, all night long, and sometimes for a few nights at a time. Some nights were during the week, and it didn't matter if it was a school night; we'd be out until two or three in the morning.

Whenever I'd come home, I would be just as dingy.

When my mom's dates would come to the house, or she'd go out to party or gamble with them, taking me along with her. This happened often. I'd be sitting in different bars or gambling houses, eating a hot dog, and drinking a soda.

My parents partied all the time, ripped and ran streets whether they were together or apart. They were both unfaithful in their marriage. All week they'd drink from sunup to sundown wherever they were. Even though mom was an alcoholic, she could hold her alcohol better than my dad, Clifford. Even still, she didn't have time to raise children properly or take care of a husband.

My dad would be so drunk when he came home, Saran would fix his dinner, and he'd didn't realize he'd already eaten. Then he'd go to the other side of the table, swearing he didn't eat, demanding his dinner. On another one of these drunken occasions, Saran wasn't home. Instead of him going out the front door to look for Saran, he'd jump out the window to look for his wife (funny but not funny).

He wasn't home that often, but when he was home, he was very particular about me and wouldn't let anybody change my diapers. I don't know and can't explain what that was about.

Clifford was the type of person that kept people laughing. He was a crazy type of guy. My dad was my best friend; to my mind, we had a close relationship.

His hobbies were shooting pool, gambling, drinking, running the streets, and women. My mother's hobbies were gambling, drinking, partying, running the streets, and men.

My bio mom was the type of person that would do anything for you if she could. She could be very sweet, but if you made her mad, there was a price to pay. She didn't have a problem withstanding up for herself to a man or woman. She could handle her business. She and my dad fought so much after they got married that they eventually separated but never divorced.

I saw him the day before he passed away. He had a knot of money that he pulled out of his pocket. I commented on how much money he had and told him he could give me some of what he owed me.

"Nah," he responded. "I need that for my hoes."

Then he started coming on to me.

He said, "Come here, you look just like your mother."

Later, when I told that to my mom (aunt), she said, "Girl don't you tell nobody else that."

The next day, I went to get my hair done. I had a seizure while getting my hair braided. It scared the girl to death; she said she didn't know what was going on and had never seen anything like it before.

When mom (aunt) came to pick me up from the hospital, I didn't know or realize I had only half my head done.

She asked, "Shell, are you going home or are you coming to my house?"

I said, "I'm going home, Mom."

I didn't understand or ask why she bypassed the house. When we got to her house, we were just sitting and watching TV when she said, "I have something I have to tell you."

She sounded so serious. I couldn't imagine what she was going to say.

"Clifford died," she said.

"What?" I couldn't believe it. It felt as though my entire world ended. He was my life. Come to find out, the same time I had a seizure was the same time he passed.

On the day of his funeral, I was running late and didn't have time to go by his house to leave with the rest of the family. They were concerned about whether I was going to get sick at the funeral, so anyone who could come came to support me. A lot of my family was close to my dad. As I entered the church, I received the obituary. When I looked at it, I said, "Oh my God! I'm at the wrong funeral!" The name on the obituary was a different name, but when I opened it, it was his picture. That's when I found out I really didn't know him. I didn't know his real name or anything about him. I then realized he had married my mother under an alias and had never gotten a divorce and married another woman under his real name.

"How can you do that to me?" I thought. "We

always laughed and joked together, just as if we were the best of friends." I guess we weren't friends at all. I was just a nut he created in the sac.

Chapter 2
Visions in the Dark

We often went to my cousin Edna's house, which was a "happy house." It was a small, three-bedroom house where anything and everything went on. My cousin would sell beer, liquor, and dinners (my favorites were fried chicken, pig feet, and neck bones). The house had no place for children. At times I would go there with both moms, but most of the time, I was with my bio mom.

My cousin Edna once threw lye in her husband's face when she got mad at him, so when there was a houseful of people (which was most of the time), she could easily have whatever man she was seeing over and her husband not know it, because he was blind from the lye.

As I said, it was no place for children.

My mom would dress me in my nice, pretty dresses. My cousin Edna's husband Robert and our cousin Bulky and other men and friends of family would all do similar things to me. If I was sitting on the sofa, they would put their toes and fingers up my dress and fondle me. I didn't like it. It was painful and felt strange. I don't know why no one ever noticed what was going on. I was only a few feet away. Or did they notice and not care? Later, when I'd get sent to bed after being on the sofa for a long period, the men would come upstairs to the room where I was. The lights were off, and I'd be crying because I was scared. I would see a shadow in the dark, then feel their rough hands touching all over me. Oh, it hurt so badly.

Silent Tears I've Cried by Shelly Knox

They didn't realize nor care that someone might've been with me already just before they got there. They came to do whatever they wanted to do to me after using the bathroom. It didn't matter what bedroom I was in; they made sure they'd come and find me, the baby, in the house. And they'd do whatever they wanted to do to me.

My cousin Rocco also babysat me at times, even though he always teased me and laughed at me about how black and ugly I was and how I had no business being in the family. I still considered him my family, and he'd say the same about me even to this day. When I was older, I was able to put the pieces together. I couldn't understand the reason why he insulted me so much when he saw me. It was because he really wanted me. That's why he'd always tell people that I was his "dick sucking bitch," even though I was only a baby. He was abusing me when he was supposed to be watching me, playing patty cake or potty training me, teaching me how to walk, say my ABC's, or knowing which utensils to eat with.

I was always in pain and wouldn't stop crying. I felt the tip of his penis on my tiny lips while he was shoving his genitals in my mouth, past my little gums. My mouth wasn't big, and he enjoyed shoving himself in my mouth. I felt as though I was choking while the walls were closing in. I felt nothing but pain throughout my body as he kept shoving my head into his genitals. The more I tried to pull away, the more he forced himself into my mouth. I don't understand why my mother would leave me with him.

I continuously ask myself that, even still today. Later, when I became an adult, he and I were close. One day, I was bragging about my baby's father, and he said, "I don't know why you're bragging about him. That pussy was mine when you were 15 months old until you were 5 years old. That's when I had fun with you. I always watched you."

Who does that? Who says that?

That's when I became distant from him, even though we had been close before that. If someone tells you they raped you, believe them. The others I remembered. These types of things went on for a long period, years of a lot of different men sexually harming me—always and at any time. This trauma caused me to have problems not only in school, but throughout life. I was in pain and cried all the time

Silent Tears I've Cried by Shelly Knox

and had trust issues. I couldn't focus on life or school; my attention span wasn't good. When I'd gotten older, I had sex issues and would give anything to be loved by anyone growing up. All I ever wanted was to feel loved.

My family would give me beer and alcohol when I was three years old. Hoping that would put me to sleep or change my behavior. By 12 years old, I was drinking on my own to put myself to sleep.

Rocco always got away with his dirt. He slept with the daughters of both his girlfriend and aunt. One of them had twins and they looked just like him. He also has a son/grandson who was born with autism by his daughter. I guess he didn't really get away with anything because God sees all.

He and the rest of the family always made me feel so ashamed of myself. My self-esteem was very low, and I thought very poorly of myself. I always ran away, and I tried to commit suicide over thirty times by taking massive overdoses. My mother (aunt) even said I should've never been born, that my mom had no time for me, and I was just an ugly child, the darkest and most unattractive thing that the family had ever seen. Even my classmates and almost everyone I ever came across always looked at me as being very unattractive and slow, and they didn't have a problem telling me this either. Not only was I bullied at school, but at home as well. When being bullied, especially at home, you begin to believe all the negative things that you've been told. I was the only black sheep in the family. No one ever wanted me around, besides a few cousins my age and one or two aunts and two uncles.

That's it. I never had hugs. No one ever said I love you. No one ever told me I was pretty and the saying "a face only a mother could love," certainly didn't apply to me. I had questions and needed answers. Where was the love?

Because of you, I am me, because of
Christ, I've made it. God promised

Silent Tears I've Cried by Shelly Knox

me: Don't worry, I have a plan. Just leave it to me.

After I read a book, I couldn't tell you what I read and still can't to this day. I can't understand or remember the simplest things. It was always hard to pay attention (focus) in class, because of all the trauma I'd been through as a child.

I was also overweight as a child. All I wanted to do was eat. I wouldn't even be hungry. When we'd go to New York, Uncle John Jr. always cooked a large spread. On one day, I ate so much I was about to bust. With my stomach hurting and all, Mom said, "Don't you eat anything more tonight. I'm going to beat you if you do. Now go to bed."

Everyone else went to bed. Uncle came home and worked his way to the kitchen. I snuck in there with him. He was eating and asked me if I was hungry. I asked him if I could please get some of those biscuits and gravy.

Mom came in and said, "I thought I said nothing else to eat!"

(He made the BEST biscuits. Great memories!)

The next day, Aunt May came over to take me to spend the day with her grandkids. They were older than me. Auntie bought a chocolate cake for my cousin's birthday party, and I just knew I was staying for the party. Auntie said, "Come on, Shelly, let's go! I got to come back in time for the party." I thought she was going to cut me a slice of cake. Well, she didn't. It took me forever to put my coat on, and before I knew it, I stuck my hand in the cake. When Auntie came to get me to put my coat on, she saw a hand full of chocolate cake. She tore my butt up. Auntie had them long fingers that curled up on the end; they hurt worse than the belt. Then she went and got the belt. That's why I still don't like chocolate cake today.

Chapter 3
Nights I Cried

There were many days and nights I cried and cried, not only because of fear, but because of pain and not having a place to bear or anyone to care.

People were so mean to me. I often looked in the mirror to see why they had so much hatred for me. What could I have done for them to beat me up with words or tear me down physically? The few friends I had stood by my side. As a child, I was always known as fat black Shelly in school and in my family as well. The family were just as bad as my classmates. My family had no idea what I was going through in school and dealing with other abusive family members, not that it would've mattered.

I always hid the pain by laughing or cracking a corny joke to make people laugh. I was always threatened in school because of my appearance. They'd say I was so ugly and got beat up every day. Then of course at home, being told the same things every day, that I was so ugly I should've never been born, along with all that name calling

Silent Tears I've Cried by Shelly Knox

and beating up. All I could do was to hate myself for being born. If I could change myself, I would. My jokes were so corny; I tried hard to fit in everywhere. The more I tried, the more I felt out of place. I didn't know how to communicate with others and still don't. People don't know how to take me. Sometimes they take me the wrong way. Sometimes I come off the wrong way when I don't mean harm.

I wanted so much to be loved by my family; I wanted to be a part of them in the worst way. It didn't matter how much I was going through or hurting. Strange how life goes when you're taught by people that are supposed to love you the most. You're not so outside, and your inside is ugly.

Life was a challenge for me. The pain was severe. Being alone made me weak, and nobody knew what I was going through. It was hard to focus on me, on my life, and the things I had to do for myself.

Philippians 4:13 I can do all things through Christ who gives me strength. All my childhood (every day). Never let anyone belittle you. Look to God for all answers.

The pain was unreal. The feeling of being rejected and not accepted is painful. Being stomped on (physically) is a painful experience. Being lied about is a painful experience. Family and friends using and abusing you is a painful experience. It's painful to be mistreated when all I ever wanted to do was to be loved by you. It's painful to be with me.

The days and nights I were in so

much pain, I never knew that one

day I'd be saved. He saved me and

set me free from all the pain and

misery. No one knew or ever could

imagine what my day was like on a

daily basis. Thank God for saving me.

Yesterday was gone. Tomorrow isn't

promised (maybe too late). Today's

memories can last forever. You're to

love yourself first.

Silent Tears I've Cried by Shelly Knox

Every year after school ended, my aunt (mom) would take me clothes shopping for the summer, so I'd have everything I needed to go down south. Each year, I went down south for a summer vacation. I really looked forward to that time, spending the summer with Uncle Tip and Aunt Helen. Acting like a kid seems like a good idea sometimes. I had the option to play and explore the yard, pick and eat berries, and enjoy a swimming pool on the property. I had friends, and I went to camp where my auntie worked at the school. She cooked, and everyone loved her cooking. I was there with her at school while she was working. I would act up, so they got me a babysitter. Ms. Elena didn't play. When I'd act up over there, I would get beat with a switch and after lunchtime, I didn't understand why I had to lie down and take a nap. I thought it was punishment. Then Ms. Elena would tell my auntie, and I got another beating with a switch.

Down south, they believe in giving beatings with switches. My uncle wouldn't beat me, but my aunt did. I would act up at my aunt's house from time to time, banging my head on the walls, having tantrums, and passing out on the floor. Aunt Helen would say, "go get me a switch off that tree." When I wasn't getting switches off the tree, I was busy eating the black berries off of it. The worst that happened to me while being down south was being eaten up by mosquitoes.

They took good care of me. While I was down south, Aunt Helen always made sure my hair was done by one of my cousins. I was very tender headed, and they hated doing my hair just as much as I hated them doing it. I always cried and wouldn't keep still.

My aunt and uncle always took me to the fair or Ocean City, Maryland. When my aunt took me to New York with her when she'd go away for the summer, they took me to Coney Island. I never saw anything like that before. I really enjoyed myself. But, when we were there, I acted up the worst. My cousins told me to give their mom a rest and not to visit the following summer, because my behavior was terrible. By this time, I was staying with the Johnsons, and my mom called and told me my auntie had passed. When I got older, my cousin asked me why I used to bang my head up against the wall and have tantrums when I couldn't get my way. I tried to explain to her what a lot of people

Silent Tears I've Cried by Shelly Knox

didn't know that I had a lot of trauma in my life as a child that I was dealing with. I didn't know how to cope with or deal with the issues I had going on in my life. A lot of people didn't know because they had never seen me go through anything. All they knew was there periods of times when I wasn't around.

*"I've learned that people will forget
what you said, people will forget
what you did, but people will never
forget how you made them feel."*

~ Maya Angelou

*Trust within the Lord, I don't know
where I'd be without his grace and
mercy. Don't let your family down.
They're counting on you. They need
your love and support. It was meant
to destroy me. I overcame it. You
never know how strong you are until
being strong is the only choice you
have.*

Even though I had people by my side, no one ever

really knew what I was going through or ever really understood why. Neither did I. No one knew what I'd been through already. As bad as my behavior was, they just wanted me gone, no questions asked. I always felt alone. I didn't know what to do, and I had nowhere to go, or anyone to turn to.

Love is something that's free. You should never have to pay or beg for it. As a friend or family member, I should be able to come to you and talk to you about anything without being humiliated, talked about, or made to feel some type of way. I should be able to cry on your shoulder and it be okay. If I must beg, borrow or steal your love, then it's not really love.

My brother was 11 years older than me, and he was so loved by family. That was what was important to me, not the materialistic stuff. Saran gave him love. That's what I didn't have. I had to learn to live with it. If you don't have love or know Jesus Christ as your savior, then you don't have anything.

When a child has the types of problems and behaviors I did, parents should be concerned about trying to fix the problem instead of trying to get rid of the child. That type of behavior isn't normal and shouldn't be ignored, not unless there's no love for the child. Parents or other adults should communicate with the child and ask what's going on in their life. Adults should believe what children tell them and not doubt or disbelieve what they say. They should ask why and pay attention to the child's answers and behavior. I needed some type of counseling. The complaints about my behavior were to see about getting me out of the home, not to solve my problems. My brother got away with cutting up my sneakers and destroying and hiding my clothes so I couldn't go to school. I had to deal with all of this. It was rough on me and, of course, my mom (aunt) believed my brother over me. No one knew at the time all that I was dealing with. Some days I skipped school, just to get away from it all.

I didn't know that I should tell a police officer about what was going on in my life, or to mention it to someone at school. I already felt terrible and embarrassed about my entire life and the situation. I needed assistance. After telling my mothers and they didn't do anything, I thought nothing else about it.

No one had any love for me, ever.

Everyone in the family had nothing but love for each other. Not me. My mom (aunt) worked nights until she retired. After 30 years, she started a boarding home business. There were often big parties there. My mom took care of mostly elderly and residents with mental health issues. These clients were provided three meals a day, medication, and their clothes were laundered, all done by the caretaker of the facility. While running the business, family members and friends of the family would sleep with some residents. By me seeing this, I thought it was okay for the residents to touch on me. They were touching me, and I thought I liked it. I thought it was okay because my family and their friends had done the same thing to me.

The caretaker slept with some residents as well. There was only one room for the caretaker to sleep, so when I stayed there with my mom (bio) and her men, any of her male friends would sometimes come over. She would send me to bed. In a lil while, she'd come to bed when she thought I was sleeping. Not long after she came to bed, her man friend would get in the bed as well. It appears my mother was asleep, so he got on top of me first and penetrated me, then I started making too much noise because it was very painful. After he took care of his business, he got off me and then got on top of my mother. They both kept moving a lot and making all kinds of noises. Talking about having the best of both worlds, I had no idea what was going on.

When running the home, Mom became friends with women in the church that hung out at my cousin Edna's house. Then, both my mother's joined the church. Mom found time to get me in the children's choir and usher board. My mother was in the Willing Worker's Club and sang in the choir. Even though they were in church, that didn't stop the partying.

I was such a terrible child that my mother had the pastor talk to me about my behavior. It didn't help me at all. I always had all kinds of adult activities going on around me as a child. Both mothers often had different men over and we always had family and friends over to visit wherever we lived, all day, every day. Mr. Hock was sleeping with my mother (aunt) and his son was seeing my mom, and then it would be someone else on the next visit. Also, the son was fondling me as well. Then the next time any man came over, they'd fondle me, too. Every time these men came over, they'd switch up with different partners and I'd be all mixed up in the game. Then Mr. Mack would come over and be with Mom (aunt). Saran (bio mom) would also be with Mr. Thomas. He always brought fruit from his job to give some to me and my mother. He always met Mom at her house and gave her money. I would hear noises coming from the bedroom. He always gave me money as well. Boy Ro would also come over often to see Saran. Through all this, my behavior continued to get worse. My mother never sat me down to ask why I acted this way, just like I never received hugs and kisses as loved ones normally do. I was never told I was loved.

Be thankful. This is my house. Someone else is hungry. I do have a loaf of bread. Someone else is homeless. God has put me through situations to show me that's not where I needed to be. All I can say is Thank You Father. I'm so grateful.

Chapter 4
Apologies to both my mothers, R.I.P.

I know y'all prayed for me; I hope y'all knew I loved the both of you, being that I put ya'll through so much hell. Maybe y'all didn't know how to love me. I knew you were probably worried. Please forgive me for what I put you through. I was only a nobody trying to live like somebody, but it seemed like everybody was hating me. If you took a minute, you'd see me, a person just like you. Learn to love and appreciate what you have. Just because people differ from you doesn't mean they don't need love too.

Silent Tears I've Cried by Shelly Knox

My ultimate desire was to become like you. I Wanted Hair Just Like You. I Wanted to Look Like You. I Wanted to smile like you. I wanted to fit in like you. I Wanted to Feel Happy Safe just like you

After Mom (aunt) ran the boarding home for years with the help of family and friends, she could purchase a home for her family. She bought the home because my brother got married and started a family. It was a beautiful home. It had an eat-in kitchen, a breakfast room, two living rooms, seven bedrooms, five bathrooms, a laundry room, two front yards, a side yard, a large backyard, a large, finished basement, a washroom, and an attic. There were large trees all over the yard. It was a dream house.

The family would come there and have a good time drinking and gambling. That's all they ever did besides eating. They loved to cook and eat all day, every day. Once, while they were upstairs drinking, my friends and I were drinking downstairs in the basement. This house was the hangout spot for my friends. I felt like I had no family, and my friends were the only people I fit in with. One weekend, Mom was sleeping, and I didn't know she was all the way asleep, and I asked her if I could have a party next week. She gave me an answer, and I thought it was yes. When the next week came, everybody was asking, "Shell, are you still having that party?" I told everyone I was. When Saturday came, I reminded Mom about the party.

Silent Tears I've Cried by Shelly Knox

She said, "Girl, I didn't tell you that you could have a party."

I said, "Oh my God. Now I have all these people coming."

"I don't care. No party," Mom said.

Mom went out when all these people in the neighborhood were ringing the bell and knocking on the door for the party. My friends were telling them that the party was canceled, and I was hiding in the basement with my boyfriend. My mom came home. All the people on the porch saw the headlights pulling up in the driveway and started ducking and diving in the bushes. When Mom came in the house, Ms. Mary told my mom, talking very loudly as always, "Shelly is in the basement with some boy."

Mom came down the steps and said, "Alright, alright, come on outcome out now." The guy was hiding in the closet. I was reading a magazine, sitting on the sofa.

I said, "Mom, what are you talking about?"

He came out of the closet. I walked him to the door. Everyone else had to leave too, except for Jazzy J and Lean, who both stayed the night.

We talked about that night forever.

Silent Tears I've Cried by Shelly Knox

Just Because I'm Different I Have Feelings Too I Deserve Respect Also That doesn't mean it's ok to be hateful or disrespectful Nobody's perfect, we need love to Walk a mile in my shoes See what I see Feel what I feel Then maybe you'll understand why I do what I do. Til' then, don't judge me.

Someone once told me: I sure wouldn't want to be in your shoes. Instead of feeling sorry for myself, I had to think about it. Because it shows that God was with me and stayed with me every step of the way. I'm so proud of bmy shoes. They need love too.

Silent Tears I've Cried by Shelly Knox

As a child, I had very low self-esteem. I felt as though I couldn't get anybody to love me. Being a child who was always taught I was very ugly, and I would never be anything in life, I was also told that nobody would ever want me. I started hooking up at school with different friends just to be with different boys or men. I never really had love. I was always looking for love in all the wrong places. I would lie about my age, just to be with men or older boys.

I was very fast at a young age, with me being molested multiple times as a baby and young child. I started having consented relations at 12 years old (due to me already being molested). By the time I was ten years old, I was more sexually active than most thirty-year-old women, through no fault of my own. I started working as a teenager in the work program, through the school district. I was making good money. The man I was seeing was there when it was time for me to cash my check. He'd be right there to help me spend it. I felt as though I had to pay for some people to be in my life or pay for love, not everyone though.

Since I started off at a young age having sexual relations, I was really into boys at a young age. But I was very unattractive, and no one was really into me, except to get what they wanted. I really didn't see that then. I never had anyone accept me for who I was. I had a few crushes at a young age, but none of them were ever interesting.

I met this one guy in the park, and we became friends. He was much older than me and lived with his mother. When I ran away from home and didn't have anywhere to stay, I could stay with him and his mother. Him being older, of course he took advantage of me. Even though we had somewhat of a relationship, he went out and came back whenever he wanted and had no respect for me at all. We always slept together. I stayed with him until he became abusive, but I was also being abused at home, so I'd always go to his place when I left home because I felt safe with him, despite his abuse. Other times, I had to live with men I didn't really know to be safe from the streets as a young girl.

Besides him, I never had a relationship until I got older.

When my mom sent me down south every summer, there was one summer when my cousin took me to the club. I met a boy, and I believed it was love at first sight. We kept looking at each other. Before the club closed for the night, we exchanged numbers. I came back to Philly and ran up my mom's phone bill. Every time I ran away, or Mom put me out, I was running up everyone's bill.

I got him to come to Philly to stay. My mom had her seven-bedroom house, and somehow, I got him on the third floor of the house without anyone knowing. I gave him a jar to pee in if he had to go. My friends couldn't believe it. He stayed on the third floor until Mom eventually caught him when I didn't come back to empty the pee in the jar, so he had to sit down and use the toilet. Ms. Mary was on the second floor and heard the toilet flush. When I came home, the jar was empty, and I just knew something was wrong. Of course, Mom laid me out.

I loved him. He'd say things to me I had never heard of before, like "I love you." Finally, I had found someone to love me for me. He was willing to accept me. I was willing to do just about anything to keep what we had.

After she caught us, Mom said he had to go home. I was 14 years old. When he left, we kept in contact throughout the years. Two years later, I ran away from home. I reached my breaking point. I ran away and boarded a bus to Virginia, where he lived. I cohabitated with him for a few years. Went from luxury to seeing what it was like to be poor, and I appreciated it. I became pregnant and things started to change a little. He began to hang out and come home when he was ready if he came home at all. I had to get up at three o'clock in the morning to work in the fields picking strawberries, beans, and greens for a living. I knew nothing about that type of life. Everyone else would make $80 and $90, and all I could make was $15 or $20 at the most. I used part of that to eat on the way home. What was left, he'd try to take from me, and his grandmother would lay him out.

While pregnant, I became very sickly. I was so stressed, walking the neighborhood crying all times of the night. Since he was busy doing what he wanted to do, I spoke with the people at the clinic about my situation and they asked me did I wanted them to call my mother. I thought about it. At that point in my life down south, while walking in the middle of the night. I walked by a phone booth and called my mother. I was so depressed I just needed to hear her voice. I called and hung up on her, didn't know what to say.

When the clinic called, mom said she would be glad

Silent Tears I've Cried by Shelly Knox

to have me back home. I asked the nurse how I would get back and she told me she would take me. I couldn't believe it. All the way from Virginia to Philly.

I went home to have the baby. I was in bedrest, and my best friend came to visit. We were sitting there talking and laughing when she finally said, "Okay, I'm about to leave."

When she left, I went down to talk to Mom and told her when I was laughing; I had peed on myself.

Mom said, "Girl, you're in labor."

I said "No, I'm not in pain."

Mom said, "You have to go to the hospital." She called the ambulance.

When I went to the hospital, I was in a lot of pain. The nurse said, "You're in all that pain, don't worry, you won't be delivering till tomorrow sometime." The aide took me back on the stretcher and the baby came out within an hour. He came out right on the metal stretcher.

I called mom as soon as I had him. She said, "What's his name?" I was going to make him a junior. Mom said no. Give him dad's first name and

I'm going to give him his middle name."

After his father put me through so much, she wasn't too crazy about him.

Things were different for a while in my family; the baby brought the family closer together. Then it seemed like things went right back to being the same as they always were.

My baby's father sent me money for a ticket. I went down to see him in Virginia. Things were great for a while. I worked at the potato grater, and then at Perdue, at then the clam house (I couldn't take the smell, I was nauseous and picked crabs). When he got bored and decided he wanted to mess around, he was never home.

After some time, I called my family, and they came and got me. I waited to leave until no one else was home, and I met them at the end of the road. When my baby's father left home, he had been wearing dark clothes. He had taken my keys to the house with him, so that if I left I, I couldn't get back in. I had to go back for something, so I knocked on the door and didn't get an answer, so I figured he still wasn't home. My brother pushed me through the window. When I was halfway through, I started

Silent Tears I've Cried by Shelly Knox

kicking and screaming. "Get me out! Get me out!"

My brother hurried and pulled me out and grabbed his gun and said, "What's the matter? What's the matter?"

I said, "He's standing over me with a hatchet, dressed in all white."

I was really scared.

We got out of there fast.

I went back home, and things were much better. The dating scene wasn't working out for me, so I started computer dating, and dated the first person who seemed as though he was interested in me. We started getting serious, two years after the other relationship. Things were good for a while. We were working in different hospitals. I got pregnant, and he asked me to marry him.

We started having terrible arguments, and he became very abusive. He would beat me up every other day, if not every day. On the night before we were to get married, we had a terrible fight. All our fights were over nothing or over something crazy.

"I'm not marrying you," I told him that night.

He grabbed me up by my neck and said, "You're going to marry me or else!" (I was skinny) An actual threat.

I had no other choice but to marry him. I didn't want to get my family involved, especially after they had just gotten me out of a situation two years before that. It would've been embarrassing to go through that again. I later found out that he wanted to get married, so he'd have someone to take care of the kids. His ex-wife was about to lose custody of their kids and he needed someone that would be home during the day that he could depend on. I found out later that he lost custody of one of his kids because once, when the baby was happy in the crib shaking and rattling and making noise, it was too much noise for him and he broke the baby's legs. Another incident was when Children Services came to visit the house and found the baby, at only two years old in the tub with second- and third-degree burns. Children's Services took the baby right away.

Silent Tears I've Cried by Shelly Knox

"I still tried to fit in from sunup to sundown, day to day. It was painful to see the hurt within me. Felt as though my insides were torn apart. All I could do was to cry 'til the tears were gone. Then I cried without no more tears. The pain remains the same."

"You made fun of me; *You never knew what I was going through, nor did you even care. We are blood and even better we once were friends. What about me? I laugh and I smile. Even when I'm hurt, I cry when I'm alone. I love everyone and trust too many. I make mistakes.*"

Chapter 5
Family Gatherings

We had large gatherings from time to time. After the older crew passed, the family grew apart, but the gatherings became larger. The family wasn't what it used to be. Everyone used to have love for each other. Now everyone was in their own clique. If you didn't fit in, you were like an outsider. I was always outside.

A few years after my brother's divorce, he planned a big wedding in my mother's yard. I was supposed to be at the wedding, but I had run away from home two months before the wedding took place. Somebody had already taken my role in the wedding. Two weeks before the wedding, somebody stole the lawn furniture and Mom was fussing at me that she just knew I had taken the furniture.

The following week, I came into the house as usual from being out with my friends. It was about seven o'clock in the evening. Between Mom and Ms. Mary, dinner would usually be left out for me on the stove. This particular night, when I came in, there was nothing left out. It was very strange. There was no food left out, no food in the chest freezer, and very little in the refrigerator. That was odd because Mom always kept the chest freezer full of meat.

I got up the next morning as usual to go to school and didn't think to mention anything about the freezer being empty. I walked home that afternoon from school with my friends as usual. When we got to my mother's house, Mom and Ms. Mary were packing up all my clothes and belongings. I said, "Mom, what's going on? Why are you packing my things?" I kept asking variations of the same question. "Mom, if you're putting me out, can you please at least tell me why?" Why are you packing my clothes?

Eventually, she turned to me to reply. She said, "You stole all the food out of the freezer and all my lawn furniture!"

"Mom, no! No, I didn't!" I spoke.

But she didn't believe me.

I had four large trash bags of all my belongings and no carfare. I had four friends, and each one helped me with my belongings, since Mom took me out and I had nowhere to go. I talked to our friend

Deloris. She was the oldest, and she had her own apartment. I went to ask her if I could stay with her, but she couldn't let me as her landlord wouldn't allow it. She did let me leave a couple of bags at her house while I looked for a place to stay. I could leave my other's bags at each of my friends' houses and took just one small bag with me.

My friends came up with the idea of talking to Old Man Barry, the owner of the deli, to see if I could stay there just for a night. They were determined not to go home until they got me straight. Mr. Barry agreed, since it was supposed to snow.

He gave me a cheesesteak for dinner after he cleaned the restaurant, and we went upstairs to where he sleeps. I was afraid and didn't know what to expect. He had a sofa bed. He went to bed and told me I was welcome to lay down and that he would not bother me. Eventually, I laid down beside him, and he didn't touch me. We got up the next morning and I could take a shower. He fixed me breakfast and gave me ten dollars to put in my pocket.

My friends came and got me that morning and asked if I was okay. I told them I was and how nice Mr. Barry had been. I thanked God for my friends.

Silent Tears I've Cried by Shelly Knox

After that night, I couldn't find anywhere to stay, so when my friend Trina's landlord wasn't home, I could sleep on her porch. I had nowhere to go to the bathroom, and I was scared to go to sleep. Some days would be raining, snowing, or just cold. Begging friends for food was starting to become normal, especially when hunger pains hit. I don't know what was worse, being hungry or not having a restroom to use.

My friends couldn't be there all the time. When they were around, I had nothing to worry about. If I had to pee in the middle of the night, I didn't know what else to do but pee in my clothes. Sometimes, I could get a plate of food or a sandwich from a friend. I went from house to house. My friend's landlord saw me sleeping on her porch and said I couldn't stay there. I walked downtown from Mt. Airy to Center City with my belongings, which was a ten-hour walk. I went to the juvenile justice center, hoping they would give me a place to stay. I was told the only way I could stay there was if it was through a social worker. I didn't know what else to do. I phoned my girlfriend, informed her of the situation, and requested that she and her boyfriend pick me up, which they did. It had snowed, so she asked her landlord if I could stay since the weather was bad. Her landlord said yes, I could, but not for long.

After being out in the street for a while, I thought about all that had happened. I called my mom and told her someone to steal all the meat out of the chest freezer and no sign of breaking and entering; they had to live there or have a key to the house. Mom replied and said that she was just so tired of me.

During this time, I continuously thought about how I had always been picked on and lied about constantly, called names, ridiculed, and bullied. I just wanted to die because I could never fit in anywhere.

Being out on the street, not knowing where my next meal was coming from, not being able to go to the bathroom or take a shower, and worrying about if someone was going to kill me, was a terrible feeling. I was so scared.

For something I didn't do. Things had gotten so bad that I didn't want to live anymore. I didn't know how I was going to make it. All I could do was just sit, cry, and wonder how my family could do this to me. What had I done to them to deserve this type of

Silent Tears I've Cried by Shelly Knox

treatment? I was so ashamed of myself.

While I was on the street, my mom was told if something happened to me, she'd be responsible. I ran out of places to go. I went to the police station, and they called my mother. For her to come, she had to be called three times. Each time she said she was on her way. The last time they called, the police had to threaten her. I went outside to her car and asked her why they had to call her three times and threatened her to come get me. I walked away and said "Mom, that's a goodbye!"

While dying inside, being homeless with nowhere to hide day and night, it was Jesus that saved me on my road of misery, trouble, and hard times. The Lord made a way out of having no way. I had a race to run, and I ran it well. I've been up and down, and falsely accused, and they'll never apologize. When I woke up, I knew that the Lord was providing for me and blessing me with such loving friends. I wasn't home, yet my brother was looking for me to nitpick, criticize, and tease. He ran into some friends of mine and asked if they had seen me, and said, "you know that Bitch is homeless."

He still found ways to nitpick, even when I was

homeless. He called the number to the phone booth near where he knew my friends and I would be at, outside of the corner store. That's where we hung out at, and I slept on the porch not far from it. Or, once my girlfriends said I could come stay with them, he'd call there and terrorize me just to let me know he was the better child.

Ok, you proved you're the better child, and you got me put out in the street. Does it make you feel better? Not knowing whether I was okay, if I was hungry or not (which I was)? I'm your sister; don't you have a conscious or even care?

While being homeless, you just think constantly about your family, how you miss them, missing my favorite meals mom would fix, things they take you through along with the pain. There were times on holidays or birthdays when I was on the street, with no family. Nothing to eat, nowhere to sleep. It was just another day.

Silent Tears I've Cried by Shelly Knox

"I do not trust people who do not love themselves and yet tell me, "I love you." There is an African saying which is: 'Be careful when a naked person offers you a shirt."

~ Maya Angelou

Chapter 6
Mrs. Lou

The mother of one of my friends heard about my situation and got permission from my mother to take me in if I was okay with it. I was fine with it. My mom paid for her and brought me my clothes while I was there. Ms. Lou was the sweetest person, and the family treated me as if I was part of the family. She would make and sell baskets and flowers on certain holidays, and she taught us all how to make money. I really appreciated that and the fact that she took me in when nobody else would. Because I was homeless, and always treated so rotten, I didn't know what it was for someone to be nice to me.

While I was staying there, my brother called a couple times, playing on the phone teasing me. Once, I ran up Ms. Thomas's phone bill, talking to the guy I had met down south, and my mom paid the bill. I was too far gone, and too much into boys already at 15 years old. I need to thank ya'll and your mom (R.I.P.), who I will never forget, for taking me in off the streets when no one else would and making me feel at home. Ya'll gave me food and shelter when no one else would. I will never forget that I was freezing, hungry, and didn't have anywhere to turn. I went to another friend's house, then continued to go back-and-forth home. Then I started staying with a guy named Don. I wasn't used to this type of environment: mice, rats, roaches, broken windows, walking around with blankets because it was cold due to the gas and/or the electricity being turned off. But it was nothing like being home. At home, I might have been able to get a home cooked meal, but at Don's, I didn't have to fight, be threatened, and wasn't called names. Most of the time at Don's, we had Chinese food, because it was reasonable. Sometimes we'd order something from the corner store.

I left Don's a few times and eventually left for good.

Chapter 7
Miracle

I never looked for sympathy. You can't look for something you never had. I regret nothing in my life, even if my past was full of hurt and humiliation. Sometimes, I look back and smile because of the way my past made me into the powerful person I am today. I'm not ashamed of anything. Even though I was traumatized all through my childhood and hurt all of my life, and until this day, people still say and do things to hurt me, and don't even know or care anything about me or my life . . .

Sometimes, we don't realize how blessed we really are. I'm not going to complain, I just want to say thank you Lord for blessing me through this terrible time.

A dream house, only for the family

My classmates couldn't believe that was my mother's house. I say all that to say; you have all that house and yet never have a place to stay. Thirteen to seventeen years old, I was always put out of the house.

Meanwhile, my mom (aunt) made sure we were always prepared for school, with designer clothes and shoes. Once I got older, I realized that was just materialistic stuff. If you don't have love or know Jesus Christ as your Lord and savior, you don't have anything. I had everything else a child could want, except for love.

God had me. The price I paid for the
life I lived. He died for you and me.
He saved me and set me free.

Silent Tears I've Cried by Shelly Knox

My brother Mitch got away with everything he did. When he'd act up, he never got sent back to stay with Saran. No one ever saw anything he did, unless Mom had a party, and he stole money out of her account to buy himself a stereo system. When we were growing up, he nitpicked a lot. He always got away with cutting up my shoelaces, taking my coats and clothes, sometimes cutting them up so I couldn't go to school. There was a time when I didn't go to school, and he tried to play the role of being my father after I was told by my mom that I didn't have to go to school that day. I got tired of him, always nitpicking whenever he wanted, so I went in the kitchen and got a knife and snuck it upstairs. He told me that I was going to school, anyway. I took my time getting ready. He came upstairs to my bedroom, threatening me, so I pulled the knife at him. He told me I had better be gone before he caught me. I tried to make it to the door, but he caught up with me and kicked me all over from head to toe with steel toe boots. I treat a dog like this. My uncle told him he can't nitpick and act like my father at the same time. There were times I did play hooky from school, but not on this day.

Even though I had people in my corner, no one ever knew everything I was going through or ever really understood why. Neither did I. Why was this happening? I was alone. I had nobody but my friends, but we were only kids.

God's work. How Did I Survive? I had nobody but God on my side.

I was always afraid of the dark. I had no idea who was going to come and give me pain that night. How sick and pathetic can a person be? I was only a child. I had nothing but pain and misery for most of my childhood. Some of my cousins say my brother didn't do anything to me. Had it been her child or grandchild, I bet things would've been different.

I learned to live and deal with it. I was known as a problem child. They never knew why I had terrible temper tantrums, falling out spells, and banged my head on the wall and floor. No one wanted to deal with the consequences of everything that had happened to me. I wasn't behaving like the average, normal child. With a child having these types of behavior problems, a parent should be concerned about or pay more attention to the child, or seek medical treatment and get help as soon as the child start having a unique behavior pattern. I was never asked by a therapist if anyone was touching me or doing things that shouldn't be done. This type of behavior isn't normal and shouldn't be ignored. I needed some type of counseling. They were more concerned about getting me out of the house instead of getting me help. When I did start

Silent Tears I've Cried by Shelly Knox

to see a therapist, it was for placement and not treatment. Just automatically, they'd say you're crazy and needed to be placed. Problems like this will get worse if they are ignored and not treated.

I was five years old when I started complaining about the men. I'd complain and my mother said to just stay away from them, that I didn't have to go around them. So, of course, it kept happening. Nothing was done about it, so I figured it was okay to keep happening with different men (family and friends of family). They kept touching and kissing me all over, forcing themselves on me, and fondling me.

Chapter 8
Melissa and David

Friends of the family, they were better than family. He and his wife had five kids together. He would come by and visit us from time to time, so he asked my mom if I could come to his house and spend time with his kids. Because the environment I was in had no place for a child, I would go there and just have a ball. All the kids in the neighborhood were always there, and they treated me as if I was part of their family. I would go over there and do things that a normal child do. We'd go roller skating, had picnics at the park, went to the movies, just things normal kids did. Church, swimming, and we even got wet in the fire hydrant. His wife kept my hair done. She was always cooking, doing other girls' hair, and making sure that all the children in her care were taken care of. When it was time to leave to come home, I never wanted to. I was over there just about every weekend in the summer when I wasn't down south. Sometimes it would be three or four of us in a twin bed. I was just as happy. I had no complaints, even if somebody peed on the bed. We didn't always get along, but we were close. My family didn't know when to come and get me. Every child should be raised, such as Melissa and David raised their children. I can't thank them enough for allowing me in their family and letting me do things that normal children do.

I'm very sorry for the problems I caused their household. By me being around all adults all the time, I would go over there and run my mouth, not knowing what I was talking about, causing problems in their home. Melissa asked who did my hair, and I told her it was David's girlfriend. Of course, David got mad at me, and my weekend was cut short. It was a while before I could go back over there again. I *had* to get back over there, as this was the only house where I was treated as family.

At home, I could play with kids in the neighborhood at my mom's house. But when I went into the house, that's when adult things started over again. I never had a childhood.

But at Melissa and David's, it was great. I can't thank ya'll enough for being there for me. Demons would speak to me as a child. After all the trauma I'd seen, these demons would tell me crazy things and put images in my head that made me believe I was crazy. They had me believe terrible things about myself. The vision would be the same exact things that had happened to me, but I would picture my mouth on another person because I was told it was okay, that this was supposed to happen to your body.

When he touched my body, he killed my soul.

People don't know or understand that when, as a young girl or an infant, you go through tragedy such as I did; it takes a toll on your life and not just at that moment. It takes a toll on your entire life. I had to fight against these grown men at an age where it was impossible to defend myself. Because of that, it was a challenge to live a successful life, or any life. After that, it was a challenge to have a normal life. That's something that sticks with you forever. In life, we must learn to forgive so we can move on, but not forget. Some of these men were 150 to at least 350 lbs. I was a child. Because I was so young, starting as young as 15 months old, and throughout my entire childhood, it caused my behavior to change. Besides the temper tantrums, I cried and cried because I was in so much pain. They couldn't figure out why I cried so much.

Certain memories always return. I was always

Silent Tears I've Cried by Shelly Knox

afraid to sleep in the dark. It was not telling who was going to jump in the bed with me that night and call what they were doing "making love" to me. They enjoyed themselves and left me with a lifetime of pain and misery.

It was like a child running in the dark, who doesn't know where to stop and doesn't know when it's going to end.

People make judgments, not knowing what you've been through or are going through. Because of this trauma, I became suicidal and didn't like my family or myself at all. When you go through this type of trauma, these are the symptoms you sometimes have. What helped me the most was years of counseling and a relationship with God. God helped me, laid his hands on me, and stayed with me the entire time. I was in the dark when I began to know the words of prayer. I prayed. I prayed and prayed for things to come to an end.

Trauma and abuse were all I was ever taught. I was taught to walk up to a man and pull his zipper down on his pants, as if I was going to perform oral sex at five years old. If this is all a child is taught, this is all a child will know. I was humiliated and judged, and people that were close kin didn't even know me.

There were some that did know, but they judged me anyway, and others who didn't. I was called all kinds of names like "whore" and then judged when I was homeless. My family hated me so much, and I hated myself.

Even though I lived an unhappy life and was hated so much, I could smile from time to time. I was very much ashamed of myself because I always felt dirty and ugly. How could I not feel that way, when that's what I was told all my life? All I needed was love, which didn't cost anything. Most people I came across, especially when I was grown and realized I didn't know how to communicate with people (and still don't), didn't understand me. I did everything I could to fit in, but all I did was embarrass myself. I tried too hard, and people often thought I had a problem. All I could do was cry and tear myself up inside and pray one day for it to be over. I never learned communication beyond abuse. Now as an adult, I still don't understand so much. I laugh a lot or tell corny jokes to fit in.

When people see you, they never see the tears behind the pain the pain behind the hurt the hurt behind the scars the scars behind the years the years behind the fears the fears in my heart are now gone, so now you can look in front of me and see me smile, with happiness. Now I walk with a broken heart and a smile that glows in front of me. If you don't know, don't say it didn't go on. Because you didn't see it Don't call me a liar Because you don't know Don't let it keep happening Because it's your family or close friends Don't keep putting me in the same environment Because you want to party Don't just overlook things Because you can't handle the situation or the truth Don't say you forgot Because you're not trying to remember Because I'll never forget (you).

I always went to church with the kids in the neighborhood, and we even went to Sunday school. I always went to the store after church with the kids in the neighborhood and could never buy anything. Mom made sure she only gave me a $1.00. We lived next door to Deacon Peyton, the deacon of the church. The church was right across the street from my mom's house. The kids in the neighborhood always went to his house to get candy. I wrote in his car one time, but he didn't tell my mother. He beat me himself. I never did that again. My mom gave me a dollar to put on the collection plate at church every Sunday. One Sunday, I was determined to buy candy from the store. When the collection plate came around, I put my dollar in the collection plate and took out four quarters.

Deacon Peyton said, "Shelly, are you going to put anything in for church?"

I said, "I did. I put a dollar on the plate."

He says, "No, all you did is get changed for a dollar."

I had no idea a dollar equaled four quarters. When I saw him years later, after I grew up, he reminded

Silent Tears I've Cried by Shelly Knox

me of that, and I was so embarrassed.

A child that struggles has no one to talk to, has no one to laugh with, has the need to be afraid, has no burdens, but is a burden has nothing but family, yet is so all alone has tears because of pain has no self-esteem has a path with no direction.

Chapter 9
Mr. V (Latin Teacher)

My mom gave me money for school. I often tried to buy friends even if it meant I couldn't buy lunch that day and would have nothing to eat. I would get extra money whenever I could just to give it to people, so hopefully they would like me that day. One day, nothing was working. I was having a bad day. I couldn't understand my work and just couldn't focus on class. I burst into tears and went into a rage. Thankfully, my Latin teacher was there. He and I went into the coatroom, and he dealt with me and my problem one on one for the longest time. I felt so close to him after that, and I was very grateful. He didn't have to do what he did. He was only my teacher. My family didn't even care. No one but him ever cared. Even now, 40 years later, he's still beside me, in my corner.

Thank God for you!

During going through the trauma in my life, when I

couldn't sleep (day or night), I was often in heavy dark places with what felt like dark clouds over me. There were times I needed to cry and couldn't. I was too afraid. I was lost and stayed lost for a long time. I had too much pride to beg for money or food unless I was around my friends. Sometimes they just knew. They would say, "Girl, I know you're hungry!" Other times, I would ask them. So many times, I had no other choice but to look at myself and my life and wonder how I was ever going to get out of the situations I was in.

Love who hates you and always pray for them. Always remember you come first. You must love yourself.

Chapter 10
Apology Alex

At first, I was sorry that we didn't get to spend that much time together. I always wished I was as close with my other family as I was with you. I will always love you. I can't forget what you did. You always had negative things to say about our father, but I had nothing to do with the way he treated you. I loved you; I didn't care about your lifestyle. You say our father was closer to me, but I didn't even know his real name. But you threw this in my face from time to time. I'm trying to be close to you. Life is too short to dwell on something neither of us can control. At first, I thought you and I were close, but when you told my son before he got out of jail that he could stay with you at your apartment for three months, as long as he went looking for a job, it didn't happen. He was there for only a little over a week. Once you realized you didn't have your privacy, then you got me in the middle of y'all's situation, cussing and fussing at me. I didn't have anything to do with it. My son is grown. Just say you didn't want him there, and that's that. That's my son, of course. I came to get him and his

Silent Tears I've Cried by Shelly Knox

belongings so he could get himself situated. You tried to make things bigger than they were. Then you started by calling me names. I was talking calmly to you, which made you madder. You said negative and childish things about me to my son. The worst part about the situation was that your great niece and great nephews were just getting to know you. They loved you.

To experience this from your hurt. I felt like anyone I loved lied to me. You were 11 years older than me and had a nonchalant attitude. You were always hot headed, even growing up. I've always loved and admired you. You weren't afraid of anything or anyone and could always hold your own. You were the first to take me trick-or-treating, to the movies, swimming, and to an amusement park. If one the of kids in the neighborhood were to hit me, I'd come in crying, and you'd make me go back outside to hit them. When Mom wasn't around, you had to do my hair, get me ready for school, and pick me up from school, too. You always made the nicest pigtails in my hair. You made me my favorite, a mayo sandwich with milk or Kool-Aid, and sat me in front of my favorite TV shows, before you helped me with my homework. These were the times I appreciated with you. When you found out through the kids in the neighborhood that the guy around the corner raped me, you went and beat him up and came home and beat me up, too. You stood up for me when I was molested by him, but you fussed at me because I didn't tell you, but I didn't know to tell you. I was always taught that it was okay for that to happen. I was told by adults to just "stay away" from men who harmed me, and then the men themselves always told me not to tell. I didn't know better. You couldn't tell me I didn't have the best brother in the world, even though eventually you didn't like me and mistreated me. I didn't care. I loved you when I didn't know how to love myself. Mom spoiled you very much, and you were very well liked by everyone. I was jealous of you being older. Mom always said, "This is my handsome young man." Nice things like that were never said about me. All the attention was focused on you. I know God makes things happen for a reason. Sometimes I look at myself now and wonder, did God have me go through these things as a child to help someone else? There have been many cases since I've grown up that I could do so. But nobody knows what I went through but God himself. And the Lord knows it wasn't easy.

You and other family say I might've been through

Silent Tears I've Cried by Shelly Knox

what I say I went through, but that I should just get over it. How selfish is that? It's not that easy. Without knowing all that a person has been through (and still going through from time to time), how can anyone say that?

Even now, there are often functions or events where I wonder why and everyone else was invited and not me. The only time I'm included is if someone they do want their lives near me and needs a ride. Why invite me to family gatherings if you really don't want me there? I've been looking for a family I could call my own, one that wouldn't criticize or judge me, someone to love me for me and look past what they see on the outside, to see how true I can be.

Chapter 11
Apology Mitch

I'm sorry to you because I feel like I could've been a better sister. I made your life miserable, and I embarrassed you. I was never on your level. I could never hold a conversation with you. I was always intimidated and nervous talking to you because of this.

It was hard to understand you. You went to Harvard, and I graduated from high school.

I don't look anything like you. I was such an embarrassment and a misfit. I wasn't the hip sister. (I was slow.) Then my seizure medication made matters worse. I am grateful for the times you saved my life.

After the passing of mom, I kind of knew there was going to be a separation.

I was never invited to you and your wife's house for a holiday dinner or gathering, so I knew I really wasn't wanted around. I was staying at the Napa Street house. I spent Thanksgiving Day alone. Mom would've never allowed that, not when she was living. No one would ever be alone on any holidays, especially on Thanksgiving. But you have your own family. I'm just so used to how mom raised us, as she did with good values.

I didn't know it until I got older, but my attention span and memory wasn't the greatest because of the trauma I had been through as a child. Even though you didn't know what I was going through, I always thought all families were supposed to be like the Johnson and our Williams cousins. For years, I've asked you for an apology for how you treated me and made my life a living hell. You've never admitted to me or Mom what you did as far as stealing the food out of freezer and blaming me, when I got kicked out of the house for it. You told me that was so many years ago and you weren't apologizing for that. That one particular time you were moving me to Virginia, I explained to you most of what had happened to me when I was younger, the different abuses that I had gone through that happened at the same time you treated me how you did. You were abusing me as well. When I told you this, all you could do was cry. I had never seen you cry before, so I took that as an apology. The only thing I wished is that you had told Mom before she passed. Before Mom passed, she asked you and you told her no. She went to her grave thinking bad things about me, but you did tell Cousin Edna. Mom knew how you were. I felt in my heart that she knew the truth, but she needed to hear it from you.

I thank you for many things. I believe the birth of Paul brought us closer together. Then we somehow grew apart again throughout the years. Sometimes, months and months went by, and we wouldn't contact each other. I wouldn't hear from you, and I was too ashamed of myself to call you. But I do know you stayed in contact with other family members. All I ever wanted to do was fit in with all the family, just like you. I can't blame you for not knowing how to love me. This is how you were raised, to think that you looked better, that I had no business in your life, that you were just better. Most of my life, you hated me. I felt as though you made me feel very uncomfortable and put me in awkward situations. I cried more than I smiled because I couldn't believe with all that I was going through, that you felt that way about me, too.

I felt like I had no one I could call my family, which I didn't.

I asked you to accept my apology for doing all the things I've ever done to you if I made you feel

Silent Tears I've Cried by Shelly Knox

miserable.

When mom passed, you didn't include me in making any of the funeral arrangements. You and your family really took me through so much it was unreal. I'm over that now. You and I as brother and sister, even though we're very different, we should've been able to sit down together and make funeral arrangements. I didn't want money. I didn't ask you for anything. I just wanted to be included in making arrangements for our mother. She buried many people in our family; she deserved a real nice service, planned by the children she raised. As soon as the undertaker took Mom out of the house, my sister-in-law was going in her drawers, saying what she wanted Mom to wear. This was totally disrespectful to me. That was my mother, and she was the daughter-in-law. She had to know I'd feel some type of way.

Then she pulled that trick to have a warrant sent to me by listening to a one-sided story. I could catch a ride back down to Virginia with her; I had no idea that I would be staying in the house by myself, not after Mom passed in the house.

Chapter 12 After The Funeral

You called and had the utilities turned off; the phone turned off, and the gas tank was taken away. It wasn't like they were in your name, or something had to be paid for. The house wasn't even in mom's name. I wasn't planning to leave for another couple of days. Uncle owned the house. I wasn't in anybody's way. Uncle knew I was going to be there for a few days. I don't understand.

Mitch, when our bio mom died, you forged Jr.'s name on the deed to the house. You didn't put your name; you put your son's name. Was that so when he passed, the house would go to whomever? That was more papers you had to make up. What was the point? You already had two houses and a family.

Before Mom died, you moved a crackhead into the house, hoping I would move out with my two kids. Ya'll were having sex in every room, all over the house. This woman, whoever she was, moved my things out of my room and changed things all around the house, all while our mother was very sickly. She hadn't even passed yet. On this particular day when I came home, I realized the changes that this stranger you moved into our mother's home had made, so I got mad and decided it was time for me and my kids to go, but before I left, I made sure that woman's clothes went out on the street first. I figured all that was done just for me to move out anyway, so you got your wish. I was right, because the very next day, you and your family moved into the house.

As horrible as you treated me all those years. I can't understand why you saved my life twice. You gave me CPR once after me taking an overdose and another after me having a seizure. I'm sorry, I never said Thank You!

But I never understood. Why save my life just to treat me that way? I will never understand. Then you saw how I was treated by others.

All our times weren't always bad, but we didn't realize we had family that enjoyed us fussing and not speaking to each other. Of course, as we got older, we matured and changed. From worse to better, than better to worse.

We do have some wonderful memories, and I thank

you for them.

Chapter 13
Glam Gurl

Silent Tears I've Cried by Shelly Knox

You were my best friend and always will be. You were always at my house, and we went to and from my house to school daily. You were there all the time, especially every weekend. You and Lean would come and stay. I thank you and thank God for putting you in my life and allowing me to be your babies' godmother. You were always there for me at all times when nobody else was. Mom believed you before she believed me. She'd say, "Shut up Shelly; what happened Glam Gurl?" She said it every time we were late coming in the house, or whatever had happened that day. She didn't realize we'd already got our story together.

One particular time, for about two weeks straight, we were going out to West Philly, taking Septa and going to see these boys. On Friday night, Mom said, "Okay, be in the house by 11." Of course, we were late. Messing around and being on the trolley car didn't make it any better. So, we were late this one particular night. We said the trolley car broke down, that no other trolley car could pass. So, the next night, we went out to West Philly, messing around and coming home late again, and we said it was a fire. If there's a fire, nothing can pass the trolley car. That Saturday, we said it was an accident when we were late coming home. The following week, all three things happened while we were on the same trolley car, and we were so very late coming home at two in the morning. She didn't want to hear anything from either one of us had to say. This is when we said we'd never tell any more lies. We could talk to each other about anything. Thank you for being such a good friend in my life, Glam Gurl.

Chapter 14
Lisa

You weren't my daughter, but you were my firstborn. I had you spoiled. When your mother had to work, you'd stay with me. You wouldn't stay with anyone else. You just cried, cried, and cried. Of course, I didn't mind keeping you, because you kept me out of trouble and kept me busy. I kept you so much that you were part of my family. Mom thought nothing of you being there. Mom was giving you collard greens and cornbread when you were hungry, and the chicken bone when she thought you were teething. As you've gotten older, you became just as comical and hilarious and you love to eat at cookouts, too.

Love you

Chapter 15
Mitch Jr.

I remember when you were born. You were the cutest little guy. When your parents brought you over, I used to love to help spoil you. Then I became old enough to babysit. On one particular day, your parents needed a babysitter. I came to the projects where you lived and you were lying on the sofa asleep. It was my very first time babysitting, and I had no experience. I was a nervous wreck and didn't know what to do once I was there by myself.

I had to go to the bathroom. The apartment was small and very quiet. Before I knew it, you let out this loud cry. I ran into the living room, and you were lying on the floor. My heart was in my tail and just pounding. I didn't know what to do. I wanted to cry myself. I was nervous. I picked you up, and you got quiet. I realized I didn't see any blood, and I said to myself, "Phew. He must be okay."

I loved when I got to help spoil you. As you were younger, we were always close. By coming over to Nana's house all the time, you got to know my friends, and they loved you as well.

Your parents brought you over one day, not long after you started walking. You always loved being around me and my friends. I'll never forget this one particular day, and neither will my friends. My friends came over and stayed for a while. When we were about to leave, Mitch Jr., you said, "Can I go with ya'll?"

I said, "Let me ask mom."

She said yes, as she hardly ever said no to you. You always just knew you were part of the crew.

Silent Tears I've Cried by Shelly Knox

You were just a toddler and were slow to keep up with us. We kept turning our heads to make sure you were keeping up with us as we walked through the neighborhood. Of course, it seemed like you were getting slower and slower. No one would carry you. We just walked slow, waiting on you. We kept looking and looking back, just to make sure you were okay and make sure you weren't too far back. This day we'll never forget. There were about six of us walking through the neighborhood. We walked past a group of boys playing football in the street. You were around three years old. Suddenly, I heard crying. Everyone looked back and didn't see you. I said, "Oh my God. Where is he at?"

The boys told us what happened.

The football had come over by you, and you picked it up to throw back into the street at the boys, but you fell into the sewer. We heard you crying underground. I was so afraid and didn't see you. I said, "Oh my God, I need ya'll to help me. Where is he?"

We were all scared. All I could think of was you drowning, or the mice and rats eating you. Luckily, out of the blue, a girl from the neighborhood came over to us to help. It took about ten of us to get you out. I was scared to take you home this way and knew my mom was going to kill me. The girl who was helping offered us to take you to her house to clean you up and that she would wash your clothes. These were the best words to my ears. Janet helped me bathe you and got your clothes all pressed and cleaned up. God answered my prayers. You were all fresh. I couldn't thank her enough. If not for that, there would have been a price to pay. When we got home, the first thing you said was, "Nana, guess what? I fell in a hole."

Mom said to me, "Shelly, what hole is he talking about that he fell in?"

I said, "Mom, you know that boy be talking crazy all the time. He doesn't know what he's saying."

All I could do was say *thank you, Jesus*!

Every cousin or friend of yours I've ever met, I'd always have to tell that story. You always said, "Aunt Shelly, you know I didn't fall in the sewer."

I had plenty of witnesses. Trust me, that's just one of many memories. You grew up to be a fine young man. You were the funniest person; someone could be having a bad day, and whether you knew them or not, you'd say the craziest thing to make

Silent Tears I've Cried by Shelly Knox

anybody's day. You'd put the biggest smile on anyone's face.

I thank you for those moments.

With respect, you've always called me Aunt Shelly.

I've held onto all of my emotions for years. Now I'm letting go of the things I can't change or things that hinder my growth. Father, I chose to be in your peace. I realized I couldn't be hurt anymore.

Silent Tears I've Cried by Shelly Knox

Chapter 16
How Did I Overcome the Trauma?

Counseling, prayer, and reading the bible really helped me. I needed years of counseling. Then I realized the more I talked about it, the more it helped not only me, but others as well. Prayer and reading 23rd and 27th Psalms. I didn't know much about the Bible or the verses, but I was determined to believe and keep the faith. Some folks don't believe in God, but He saved me.

I've learned that someone may have more than you, yet they'll not like you for whatever reason. Whether it's family or whoever, don't let it stop you from doing what you have to do for yourself. You have nothing to prove to anyone because Judgment Day is coming for all of us. I was far from being an angel, but when you go through such untreated trauma as I did, for so many years, even though I was counselling (certain questions weren't asked)

Sometimes life just won't be easy. Some of my

problems were hidden.

They took me to see a psychiatrist, but they never told him I was complaining of being raped. He never asked me, and I didn't know to tell him. It was like going to a doctor for headache and saying your feet hurt. That means you'll always have the headache.

When you think you have no one to talk to, you can always talk to Jesus. Tell him all about your troubles, and he'll guide you all the way through. You must keep the faith. Don't just talk to him when you have a problem. Thank him for all blessings; learn to pray and read scriptures out of the Bible. When you go through these: "trials and tribulations," you have to realize that there is light at the end of the tunnel. Just keep the faith and keep praying.

Psalm 27:14. Wait on the lord: be of good courage, shall strengthen thine heart: wait I say wait on the lord.

Psalm 27:1-3, the lord is my light and my salvation; whom shall I fear the lord is the strength of my life; of whom shall I be afraid?

when the wicked, even mine enemies sand my foes

Silent Tears I've Cried by Shelly Knox

came upon me to eat up my flesh, they stumbled and fell.

Though a host should encamp against me, my heart shall not fear; though war should rise against me, in this will I be confident.

Psalm 23: 1-6

The lord is my Sheppard; I shall not want.

he maketh me to lie down in green pastures: he leadeth me beside the still waters.

he restoreth my soul: he leadeth in the paths of rightousness for his namesake.

Yea, though I walk through the valley of the shadow of death, I will fear no evil: for thou art with me; thy rod and thy staff, they comfort me.

thou preparest a table before me in the presence of mines enemies: thou anointest my head with oil my cup runeth over.

surely goodness and mercy shall follow me all the days of my life: and I will dwell in the house of the lord forever.

Amen.

Laugh hard, smile when you can,
even when it hurts

Chapter 17
Counseling

I read these scriptures and prayed every day, not only when there was a problem. When I woke up in the morning; I praised Him. I was thankful for every little blessing.

When I was young, I prayed constantly. As I got older, I prayed and read the scriptures.

They made me go for counseling from time to time, not because I needed help, but again because my family was trying to put me away. Once I was admitted to the hospital, I was sent to different group homes. I saw that when I was away from home; I was safer. I could seek professional help as well. When you have someone to talk to, it lets the weight off your shoulders. Your mind might be cloudy, but it's easier for the professional to talk to you and help guide you through.

Then there's group therapy. When you sit and hear others speak about their past and what they're going through, you realize you're not the only one, and that's what makes it easier to talk about. That's when I became more open about my past. In group therapy, you don't feel as bad because there are others out there that have been through much worse than you have. But first things first, talk to God about it.

Going to therapy taught me to never believe people who said I was crazy or any other negative things. Just because you're talking to a psychiatrist or counselor doesn't make you crazy. We all need someone to talk to. I would like to apologize to my children. Because I know I was not an excellent parent, not as good as I should've been. A person can only practice what they are taught. The beatings and punishments I will not apologize for because they were needed, and in the long run, you will learn to appreciate those beatings, just as I appreciate most of the ones I received. I feel as though I could've done better by making different choices of fathers. I should've stayed in school. The gambling and drinking I wished I was never been taught. There are a lot of things I should've never started, that would have made me a better parent.

No, I'm not apologizing for not getting anyone out of jail. I am apologizing for when both of you were abused by my ex. I should've done something about it. T, I should've never let your 999 grandmother raise you even though she asked me and even though you wanted to. Carl, when your father and 999 I broke up, he took you out of spite. I had to move to Virginia to keep your brother from going into the foster care system down south until we went to court. Then I stayed in court, trying to get you. I was a single mom and all of y'all dads were abusive. Hopefully, one day, you'll find it in your hearts to forgive me. I knew nothing about raising a child. It was rough being a single parent, being abused, and trying to keep my kids and myself safe all at the same time. Plus, I was trying to make sure my money wasn't going to be stolen from me. I was kind of living the life my mother had lived.

I would like to apologize to my cousins. I was an embarrassment. Now that I'm all grown up, I realize how things were in the past. By going through what I went through at an early age and beyond, I did not know what to do. These are the things taught to a child; a young child doesn't just pick up on these things and knows exactly what to do. I'm not asking you to believe what I am saying or not, just know and understand that Judgment Day is coming for all of us. I'm sorry that you may never understand or you might even think it's funny. What I was going through and why I acted the way I did, and for those that were ashamed of me, I'm sorry I couldn't be who you wanted me to be. I was never perfect and never will be. I just wanted to laugh and fit in with all the others, like everyone else. We are all supposed to be there for each other and love one another as a family. I do appreciate those family members that did love me and appreciate me.

I'm sorry that we didn't get to spend that much time together. I always wanted to be as close with you as you are with your other sister. I had nothing to do with how our father treated you. You felt as though he treated you that way because of your lifestyle. I loved you anyway, even though you told my son when he came home he could stay with you for a few months or until he got his life together. I had nothing to do with that. You put him out for no reason, which put me in the middle of the situation. You didn't realize how much privacy you wouldn't have with him staying with you. Then you started with the name calling. I thought you really loved me. These were the names I heard from my other family on my mom's side throughout the years. I never thought you felt like that about me, too. How ugly, black and unattractive I was, and how there was no way we could be related. That hurt me so badly; I came and picked up my son and his belongings. The sibling I really thought the best of me was just as bad as my other family. Life is too short to dwell on the past, but that really hurts, especially because you told my son what you thought of me. It's bad enough I had to live my life with the pain, but then you told my son. I really felt as though you cared about and loved me as your sister. I guess not.

Chapter 18
More Apologies

My cousin and Rufus (both heavy drinkers) had the house (speakeasy) all day and night. It was always drinking, gambling, and playing street numbers. It was not a place for children. You stayed in denial of your husband and Bernard molesting me. You could get my brother and me closer before you passed. Right or wrong, you always spoke your mind, but never meant any harm.

You always had a kind heart. You taught my brother and me the importance of sisterly and brotherly love. You taught us well. It didn't last long, just until he fell in love with my "sister" (my best friend).

You were the funniest person I've ever known. Just a small example: When my uncle died, we got the okay to go see him in the hospital. It was you-cousin Edna, Eula, and me waiting in the hospital lobby for over four hours. You got mad and said, "I don't wait on a living man that long. I'm not gonna wait on a dead man that long." You were always funny.

Thank you, cousin, for everything.

Silent Tears I've Cried by Shelly Knox

Mom Dit

What a blessing.

I hope this is something you already know. Your life on this earth has been a blessing to so many, including me. You never said the words "no," "I can't," or "won't." You always found a way.

Trust and believe that if anything wasn't right or had to be fixed, Mom Dit would fix it, even for folks all throughout the community. I really believe that God puts people in your life for a reason. Because without you, I don't know what I would've done. Being in your home was like a safety net.

When you took me in at 14 years old as a foster child, I was broken and bruised, but in your home, I was always treated as family by family and friends, even when the roads were rough and times were hard.

You took me into your home with no problem and treated me as if I was one of the family. I really felt like part of the family and felt loved. Even to this day, I still get invites for family gatherings on Thanksgiving and Christmas, and other events. I just feel so comfortable in your home, and y'all were always understanding.

On this journey, I've lost some family and many good friends who didn't understand or accept me and what I've been through. I didn't even understand myself. But you always accepted me.

I couldn't put the pieces together, nor did I know how things were going to end. I can't begin to explain what a blessing y'all were to me.

Thanks for being a mom that I can call my best friend.

Love,

Shelly

From My Foster Mom: I Didn't Give You Life But Your Life Gave Me You. I couldn't have loved you more if you were my very own. Thank You for the privilege of being your extra mom. Thanks Mom!

Chapter 19
The Men in My Life

The fathers of my children. I have three children, with three different fathers. All three were very abusive. As a child, I had no love, so of course when I got older, I was looking for love in all the wrong places. Every time someone told me they

Silent Tears I've Cried by Shelly Knox

loved me, I believed them. Then, when they stomped me, blackened my eye, or raised their hand to hit me, I thought it was part of love. Growing up, I knew nothing about love. All my experiences as a child, being molested young, made me grow up fast. People confused that with me being a whore or wanting these men. I didn't want them. I just didn't know any better.

Look, I was molested as a baby and child. It was not my fault. It happened way too many times to count. I was always used. Most of the time, if I agreed to go out with a guy, it was because I initiated it. Or a dude would say, "Give me the money so we can go out, and I'll pay you back when I get my check." Then when he got his check, either he'd forget, just not give it to me, or I wouldn't see him anymore. I always had to pay for love. I've never met anyone that wanted to get to know me just for me. When I came across somebody I did like, I made a fool of myself and humiliated myself. It hurts because the majority of my family doesn't believe me, but when I get close to people, I go out of my way to make sure I try to keep them as friends. That's why I end up losing a lot of my friends. I try too hard. Out of all my relationships, I never had anyone hold me and tell me they love me and actually mean it. All the men I talked to or flirted with... that's not a genuine relationship. If I'm happy with a person, I don't need anybody else. You can't knock a person for what they like. Also, it can be an appearance thing. But you can be fine as wine, then when you do get in a relationship, Oh My God, it can be the worst mistake ever. It's not what's on the outside, it's what's in the heart that counts.

For a while, I had chosen to remain single and stop settling for less. I knew there was somebody out there for me, despite what I've been through. Y'all have taught me to want to help others.

As a young child, me seeing what my mother went through and accepted at a young age; I grew up all my life thinking that what she went through was how a man was supposed to treat a woman. Also, I thought that with all the men that were having sex with me and fondling me at an early age; I thought that we were in a relationship. Of course, we weren't, but I was young and didn't know. Once I was older, I realized it was just an opportunity for them to get satisfied. As a teenager and a young adult, your hormones start to change. You want friends and a relationship. By being overweight, boys didn't look at me as attractive. In school, I was always called fat, black, and ugly. At home, I was always called black and ugly, even from the men that were molesting me. My first was Don. He was 18 years old, and I was 12. I wanted a baby. I thought I could make him happy, and we could be a family, not realizing what I was getting myself into. I knew I was too young for this guy, but I stayed with him and his family from time to time. I didn't want to go back home. His home was like living in a palace. I just wanted to be in a safe environment. Neither Don nor I was ready for a relationship. I was too young and still in school and he was just starting to enjoy his life, not ready for a commitment. When he got tired of me being there, he'd sodomize or fight with me so I would leave, and then I was back on the streets again. I was going through that at home, too. When I'd go back home, I would stay until I got tired of being bullied or molested. Other than this relationship, there was one relationship I did have (my baby's father) when I was 14 years old. As a teenager, just to have a roof over my head, I was forced to live with men that I had no desire to be with. Life was horrible; I felt terrible about myself and my life.

Chapter 20
Kelvin

I met Kelvin through a friend. Everything was wonderful for a while until I was about to have major surgery and needed a babysitter for my oldest son. He was about eight years old. I asked Kelvin if he could babysit while my mom was working. He said I had to give him $500 for that one week. The relationship was going great. But he kept repeating the request for me to give him $500 in such a nasty voice. I thought he was joking the entire time. I was always close to him and his family. I thought no more of it, and came home and talked to my mom. Then something told me to call his mother. I explained to her what happened, and she said, "Oh, I'm sorry, I should've told you."

I said, "Should've told me what?"

She said, "He is on medication, and he's not supposed to drink while he's taking his meds. When he was in college, someone put a micky in his drink." She told me what happened sometimes, that he would chase her down the street with a knife or hitchhike a ride from state to state on the bus and the family would have to wire him money so he could get back home. Other times, he would lie and steal. After finding this out, I slowly withdrew from him. After we broke up, he would still come around the house from time to time. He'd have barrettes or lotion in his hair, or a belt around his neck, and would display the strangest behavior. He came by sometimes to see my uncle or my mom. His conversations were so off, you'd think he was a different person. As I mentioned earlier, one summer when I went down south, my cousins took me to a club. I thought I met the love of my life, George. My life changed dramatically to be with this man. But I thought I finally had a family that loved me for me. I've already told the story of me and George earlier, so I won't tell it again here, but there were many ups and downs with George. We lived in a two-bedroom house with fifteen people. I learned how to cook, clean (survival). I met Carl when I started hanging in bars, which was definitely the wrong place to find a good man. When we met, he seemed to be nice. He bought me a few drinks, and we had a pleasant conversation. The bar where we met was always our meeting place. I just knew this was the perfect guy for me. He turned out to be just like most of the folks in my family or friends of the family. He was an alcoholic. A long time passed, and I hadn't heard from him for a while. I called his mom, and she told me he had been incarcerated. She gave me the info, and I looked him up in the prison system. I visited him from time to time and from prison to prison. In the meantime, his daughter needed a place to stay. Her mom would put her out sometimes because they would fight, and she was a problem child. Whatever she needed, I got for her. She didn't want to go to school and wanted to fight me, always had boys in the house, and was very disrespectful. She was on her way to school one day and called me from the phone booth crying and said she was

Silent Tears I've Cried by Shelly Knox

raped. I told her to come home so we could go to the police station. We went to the sex crimes unit. They asked me what happened, and then they asked to speak to her by herself. When they came back to speak to me again, they said, "Sorry, Ms. Knox, but since she's been here, she's told twenty different stories. We don't believe her."

Come to find out, she lied, because she didn't want to go to school. I did everything for this girl. I did for her just as if she was one of my own.

Later, once her father was out of prison, she hit me upside my head with my house phone and I had to stand outside in the rain until her father felt like letting me in the house.

I had told her if she wasn't going to do the dishes, she shouldn't use them. She said, "Bitch, if you don't shut up, I will hit you in the head with your own goddamn phone." Before I could get a response out of my mouth, she hit me upside my head with my phone. Her father stepped between us. Her mother came and got her, but had the nerve to bring her back later. I paced that floor all night until they went to sleep. I went downtown and got a restraining order, and they didn't know. I waited for them to start with their mess, and as soon as they started, I called the police. The officer took them outside and listened to them and asked me if I had a restraining order. They answered no to me, and I said, "Yes I do." They said I didn't have any papers. When I handed the officer the papers, they couldn't believe it.

So, the police officer told them both that they had to leave. They left and took the baby out of spite. After one week, I began to get depressed and had to take a leave of absence from work. Around this time, he and his daughter moved back in. After I took off work, I started having health issues. My cycle would come on, sometimes for three to six weeks at a time, sometimes non-stop, and I would lose a lot of blood with very large clots. Once he was back, he was back to beating me again. He'd beat and kick the clots right out of me. I didn't know if I was going or coming. I had to have surgery.

Eventually, he moved out. Then we moved to his mother's house not long after that. We stayed there for almost two years. Life was smooth in the beginning, but after a while, money started going missing. I would get beaten for unknown reasons. One particular time I got beaten by him was because he had introduced my girlfriend to his brother, and she didn't want to talk to him. I couldn't understand that. He always had reasons for being out in the streets, usually hustling. He took money from me without me knowing, and became a loan shark, bought and sold drugs with my money, and when it was time for him to collect, I didn't receive anything. He'd come home at two in the morning and wake me up, saying he needed the debit card because somebody saw him kill somebody and he needed two hundred dollars to pay them so they wouldn't say anything. Then there were times I was just afraid and had no other choice but to give him the money. He was very abusive. His mother took up for him so much, and he gave her hell, even though she got hit in the chest by mistake and had to be rushed to the hospital. I didn't find out until later that her husband was also very abusive to her.

I became pregnant and had to be admitted to the hospital for almost two months until I had the baby. I'd just gotten my tax refund. He'd taken the ATM card, and within that time, he spent most of that money: loansharking, tricking, and selling and using drugs.

After I had the baby, we started getting back to how our relationship was in the beginning. I was working in the hospital, making good money. I'd go to the casino with him and his mom or my family. I won big money most of the time in Atlantic City or playing cards in Philly. We became all lovey dovey. He watched the baby when I went back to work.

On one particular day, the baby needed his formula. I left the ATM card and told him to get the formula and also to get himself something to eat. When I got back home, he had his grand mom watching the baby. I asked her what time he left, and she said it had been hours.

A little over a week went by, and I got a call around eight at night to meet him up at Broad & Erie. He wanted me to meet him because he knew how I was going to react, and he didn't want that at his mother's house. He was waiting at the corner where the dumpsters were, the area he "owns." (At the age of 40, why would you claim to "own" a neighborhood or a corner, just because you have crippled people or killed them?) People in the neighborhood were definitely afraid of him. When I got to the dumpster, I had to chase him around before he eventually threw the card down on the ground and ran away. He stayed away for another two days. I was still mad, and he never got the card again after that. Eventually, we became closer, and we focused our attention more on the baby and moving. We moved, and things started going well for us. Then, what money he wasn't stealing, I was gambling. My luck had run out with the gambling.

I tried to hide my money in places I didn't think he'd look. I had to put the money in a sandwich bag and hide it, or I'd run upstairs and hide it really quick, or hide around the house. A lot of times he'd find it, especially when it was between my legs. He didn't care whether the kids had to eat or if my cycle was on. I had to actually fake having seizures to keep him from beating me. That was the only way he'd stop. Not all were fake.

His daughter needed a place to stay again because she was fighting with her mother. This was *Daddy's little princess,* as he'd call her. She could never do anything wrong. She wouldn't do any chores and nothing around the house. Every time I'd leave home, I'd come back and the house would be just filthy, with a sink piled with dirty dishes. I would always say, "Sam, can you please do the dishes?" She always swore she didn't dirty them, and her father would always believe her. On one particular morning, I got up, fixed breakfast, and made sure I cleaned up and that he saw that the kitchen was clean. We were gone all day. When we returned, the house was a disaster, including the kitchen. Soiled diapers and clothes were thrown everywhere; there were clothes on the floor and dirty dishes piled in the sink and everywhere else.

She was always babysitting for somebody. One baby she even adopted when he was young (she was young herself).

Her dad forged government checks, and they looked so real. If there was a man's name on the check, he would get a man and take him to a check cashing place or a bank where he knew the cashier, and they'd cash the check. This was a hobby, along with being a drug dealer and user with *my* money. This kept me in depression and seizures. I had to take a leave from work.

He beat me and kicked me all over. It didn't matter where I was. My life was a mess. With him knowing I was sickly, why would he be so mean. One particular night, he called and said he was coming home. I made a pot of spaghetti, the best meal I've ever fixed in my life, with garlic bread, fried chicken, and a tossed salad on the side. I even made a nice, tasty marble cake.

Silent Tears I've Cried by Shelly Knox

I realized I had no way to win. He'd be beating on me just like he was fighting a man in the street. He didn't care how hard he was hitting me. When he moved, he was beating me just as much as he was before he left.

The life I lived was like shattered glass in a dream.

When my oldest son moved to Virginia to live with my mom, he got into trouble with the boys' next door. The judge gave me a choice: either you move here and get a place to take custody of your son, or he'll be placed in the system, awarded to the state. I never heard of a court order like that. I came back to Philly when it was my weekend to get the baby (my youngest son). I decided to take my family and all of us moved to Virginia. Before I had a chance to file for custody in Virginia, Carl and his family ransacked my house, looking for anything they could find with my mother's address or phone number on it. They filed a petition full of lies. The sheriff showed up at my door with the petition, and I couldn't see who was in the back of the police car with the police. They took him, and I kept them in court for years trying to get full custody of my son. I had a close friend. We were close as sisters, and every time I had to go to court, she'd take off to go with me.

Finally, I did receive shared legal custody between me and his dad's mother.

Chapter 21
Virginia

When I moved to Virginia, my first jobs were working at the chicken plant, crab house, and clam house. Later, I took the CNA Certification from Philadelphia to the hospital there and applied for Patient Transporter. After my interview with the nurse manager of the E.R., they called me and offered me the position for $7.25 an hour. She said, "You're definitely hired, but we need you to take a course at the college while you work, and you'll get a raise."

When I finished the course and received my next paycheck, I looked for a raise. My nurse manager said, "You did get it. It was 10 cents." I worked there for quite some time, and the raises were anywhere from 5 to 10 cents. I loved my job, but it was very demanding. One person for the entire hospital was rough. Nobody ever understood why one person couldn't be in five places at a time. It was on one busy day, when I was getting calls back-to-back, and nobody understood they had to wait. I couldn't take it. I called the nursing supervisor and relieved myself of my duties. That was when I started my daycare and medical taxi service. By this time, the insurance for the medical taxi was outrageous. That's when I decided to move back to Philadelphia. Before I moved, I applied to different hospitals for CNA and Patient Transporter positions.

I'm glad that things turned out the way they did. It might've been different If I would've stayed in Virginia. But who knows? I just don't like the fact that they lied to my son, and the courts, and ransacked the house. For years, my son was brainwashed and felt some kind of way.

When I did move back home, I tried to find a place, then I finally got a job. My ex and his family were very intimidating, and he was very abusive. I waited until I moved back home before I started calling him and then picking him up to take him out.

Chapter 22
Julius

I met him back when I moved to Virginia while working at the chicken plant. At first, everything was smooth. We spent a lot of time together. Then he became abusive out of nowhere and for no reason. I just couldn't understand it. It was my birthday, and he took me out to dinner. When we came home, he surprised me with a negligee. I was a size 2x, and he bought a medium. I told him it was too small, and he beat the crap out of me and made me put it on. I squeezed into it. Then he wanted to make love, and I was very uncomfortable and crying. After that, we made up. But it was the same thing again and again, always argument after an argument over stupid stuff.

One time, I was driving on the highway, and he just grabbed the wheel and almost caused an accident because he didn't like my response to something. He called me on the job on a Sunday and asked if I had any money. I told him I didn't. He came up to the job, anyway. It was Sunday and a slow day. We were down the back hall and he chased me, trying to make me give him money I didn't have. Then he went to the parking lot and scratched my car up. My co-worker called me and told me he went over by my car. She thought he slashed my tires, but he scratched the paint off. I knew I had to stop being afraid and realized he was on drugs. He got mad and called my mother and told her that she had better talk me into going to the doctor. He claimed that while I gave him a blow job; I bit him on his dick and gave him a venereal disease. I explained what was going on to her, and let her know he was just trying to tell her that to embarrass me.

Chapter 23
Harry Stellman
(Casanova)

I met Harry at the post in Virginia on my way to another club. When I got to the post, I was depressed because I had just found out the guy I had been seeing was married. We had been getting close when I realized he was only with me to satisfy his needs. I was really hurt. I was sitting there, moping and drinking. I went outside to get some air, and this guy walked up to me and said, "Why aren't you smiling?" I didn't reply.

About a half an hour before the club was about to close, he walked up to me again and said, "You still ain't smiling." I told him, even though I had never met him before, to come with me to another club. He got someone to drive his car, and he drove my car, as I was too intoxicated to drive. We were just riding around. I fell asleep and never made it to the other club. We hadn't yet exchanged names. I had always been a hard sleeper, and he couldn't wake me up to find out where I lived. He drove by his family's house to see if they knew me. Even though it was a small town where most people knew each other, they didn't know me.

I was living at my mother's house. He got his nephew to follow us in his car so he could get a ride back home in case he did find out where I lived. As we were riding on a back road, I woke up. He asked me where I lived. When he approached my house, we exchanged names and phone numbers. As soon as he said his name was Casanova, I said, "Oh, okay. I already know you're a player with a name like that." He assured me it was just a name he was given back in school. I had to work in a few hours, so I didn't get much rest. At work the next day, I mentioned his name to my best friend and coworker, and she said she knew him.

We dated for a while. He seemed to be the perfect gentleman. I was happy I was finally dating a gentleman. Little did I know, he was already in between dating two different women. With one woman, he had to sneak out the back door or window of her house when her man came home. When he met me, she was pregnant. The other was his baby momma. He never really got over her. We dated for a while, but it took us eight months to become intimate. I thought something was wrong with him or that maybe he was gay.

We realized that his best friend Warn was a guy I had been seeing when I was a teenager. We had been very close. Casanova and I realized what a small world it was. They were both part of a domino club, men and women. I knew a little about the game because my family had already taught me how to play. I wasn't as good as they were. When he took me to meet his family, a lot of them didn't like me because I was very unattractive and overweight. We'd go to his dad's house and play spades, which was a lot of fun.

Eventually, I could get a house. One of his sisters told him, "You better move in with her. I don't care what she looks like, she's getting a brand-new trailer."

He moved into the trailer with me and my kids. He paid his rent faithfully, $400 dollars a month, and before the month was out, he got most of that back for beer, liquor, and cigarettes. Things were going smoothly for a while. I always cooked southern style meals. I was still working at the hospital, and when it was time to go clothes shopping for the kids for school, Easter, Christmas, birthdays, etc., I made sure I included his two children as well.

Silent Tears I've Cried by Shelly Knox

As time went on, I noticed that he was a big flirt. He didn't care if I was right there. I had a feeling he was messing around. As he always said, if you don't catch me, it's not me. We always had birthday parties, Super Bowl parties, and dinners. Good times.

But sometimes, he would get a terrible attitude for no reason. We weren't having sex as often as we used to, either. Maybe three, six, or eight months in between. I knew it was a problem.

Chapter 24
My first marriage: Daryl

I was having trouble coming across the right guy, so I went through a computer dating service, and they matched me up with this seemingly really nice guy. They said he was a perfect match. We dated for about six months and got along very well. We seemed perfect for each other. I mentioned him earlier, but will give the complete story of Daryl now. Sometimes, he bought me flowers just because. I told him I didn't like flowers because they die. He asked, "Well, what do you like, candy?" I told him I only liked fruit. So, he'd order different types of fruit baskets, or get fruit off the truck. This was especially true when we'd had an argument, or just because. He came off as so loving. I had never had that before. When we met, I was only 19. He lied and said he was 36 when he was 45. I didn't understand that lie for no reason about his age.

We had our basic ups and downs as all relationships do. He had four children that lived with his ex-wife. The state said the mom was an unfit mother and threatened to take the children away. Because she was never home, the utilities were off and the kids were often hungry, asking neighbors for food or trying to fry cornflakes. They were raising themselves. Matters got worse, and the state had to take them away. The state gave Daryl the option of taking the children, but he had to have someone living there with him to cook and help while he was at work. I agreed to help. We had been dating for about six months and we got along very well and seemed so perfect for each other. The kids' ages were from 6 to 10, three boys and a girl. When they came, I was really excited. I didn't know, but that's why he wanted to rush into marriage. I didn't mind; actually, I loved it. Of course, that's where things went downhill, and he started to get violent with me.

With all the cooking I was doing Sunday to Thursday, he was fine with it when I asked him if it was okay not to cook on Friday and Saturday nights. I had always wanted a big family. Eventually, I got into a good schedule, cooking every day. The first Saturday, I felt so good. I decided I was going to cook a big breakfast for everybody. When I got up to cook, I fixed the works. I made French toast, cheese eggs, pork sausage, grits, bacon, and home fries with onions. While cooking, I like to taste my food to make sure it's seasoned well. I'd just had major surgery on my stomach, and couldn't eat much. I fixed the kids nice, healthy plates, and for Daryl, a nice sized man serving. He was a very big eater. When I fixed my plate, he looked at it, and said, "Bitch, what da fuck you trying to do, poison us?"

Before I knew it, I had blows coming to my head so fast. Blind as a bat, I couldn't see anything. Of course, I was filled with rage, screaming and crying that all I was trying to do was feed my family. When I could see, I picked a little steak knife and gave him a slight cut, just enough to give him three or four stitches.

The kids were always afraid of me. I would get beat for the craziest things. If I went to visit my mother without telling him, or if a guy looked at me, in the market or while I was walking down the street, if I didn't answer the phone when he called, after two rings or I took too long coming out of a store, I'd be bleeding from the nose and mouth. I was the type of wife that didn't really go anywhere unless it was my mom's house, doctors' appointments, or the

Silent Tears I've Cried by Shelly Knox

market. I often had busted lips and bruises all over. The neighbors heard us fighting all the time, all night long. He didn't care. Our relationship was rocky, and I was totally afraid of my life. Afraid what he would do if I was to leave him. I would leave from time to time and come back. He would always buy a fruit basket and have his oldest son bring it to me.

I was pregnant, and he was pushing to get married. My mom was also telling me to get married before the baby was born, and said I better not have another baby and not be married. We had to meet with my pastor first for counseling. He asked us if we loved each other, and we said yes. At the wedding, Daryl wore a suit, and I wore a nice maternity dress. Lots of family attended, included both my mothers, Uncle Teddy, and my best friend Glamour Girl. We had the wedding reception days later at the house. A lot of my family and friends came to that, too. No one knew my pain and what I was going through. He promised he wasn't going to beat me anymore. With me being young, dumb, and crazy, I truly thought I was in love. I loved him anyway, because even if he beat me, my being abused all my life had taught me this was what was supposed to happen in a marriage.

Not long after the kids came to stay, we went on our honeymoon. I was determined to go. It was a four-day cruise to the islands. The limo picked us up from our home in North Philly and drove us to the pier in New York. He had promised no more fighting. I was going through a lot in my relationship, and I told myself I would go on this honeymoon and the first time he hit me when we got back, I would leave him.

We got back on Friday, and everything was great, though we were tired from the long trip. Early Saturday morning, he wanted to fight. I reminded myself I'd been beaten on too much and wasn't going to take anymore beatings. All day Saturday he wanted to fight and Sunday he was still fighting. He thought I was going to lay down and continue to cry as always. I got up and went downstairs and flared up on that ass. He was so shocked. Then I turned around as if I was going back upstairs, but I flared up on him again and again. He was quiet Sunday night and left home and went to work as he normally did.

I didn't answer the phone, because as soon as he walked out the door, I was packing clothes. I planned to move back to my mom's house. There

Silent Tears I've Cried by Shelly Knox

was no coming back. He had all the fruit baskets delivered and kept calling, not giving the phone a chance to hang up before he hit the redial button. It was constant. Later, he tried to kick the door in at Mom's to get me to come back home. My brother was at work, and it just so happened he was on the phone. He heard all the noise and asked what was going on and what all the noise was. I said it was Daryl trying to kick the door in. My brother took off from work to see what was going on. I was scared. I figured I'd moved on to keep incidents like this from happening.

Another time, my son was almost three years old, trying to defend me. One day, with me being pregnant and my son there, Daryl threw both of us up the steps. I was skinny. I packed our clothes, and we left and went into a shelter. When we got there, I saw how many people it was to a room, and I couldn't take it. We walked right down the street to Mom's house. She didn't know what happened until I told her when we got there.

We stayed there for a while until things calmed down. Then he started sending baskets of fruit over. We moved back in with him. He said he had changed.

Eventually, it was time to give birth. While in delivery, I was in so much pain. I had a lot of complications. He said, "baby don't worry, as soon as we get home we'll start working on more kids."

I was already crying, but when he said that, I cried the hardest. The nurse kindly asked him to leave because I was too upset. My mother- and sister-in-law came, and I was so glad to see them. He was allowed to come back the next day after the baby was born. She was underweight, so she had to stay in the hospital in the NICU, Intensive Care for newborns, before she could come home. She was so small that I was afraid to hold her. She was the smallest little baby I've ever held in my life. When she came home, we couldn't afford a crib for her. So, I took one of the dresser drawers out and padded it with pillows until we could afford a crib.

Before long, things returned to normal. I didn't go out much because I knew how possessive he was. If I would go over to my mom's without mentioning it to him, that was a terrible beating. My girlfriend called one night and asked me what I was doing that night. I told her I wasn't doing anything, and she asked me about going out. I told her I couldn't because I didn't want to have to fight when I got home. When I hung up the phone, he asked who I had been talking to. I told him it was Glam Gurl asking me to go out, but that I told her no. He told me I should go, that I needed to go out sometimes. I asked if he was sure, and he said he was and for me to call her back. My friend picked me up, and we went to the club and had a pleasant time. When I got home, he beat my tail from the door to the bedroom. Every day or every other night, I'd get beat up.

I left again with my two kids and moved back in with my mom.

Sometime later, my mom answered the door one day and said, "Shelly, there are two men at the door dressed in suits."

I went to the door, and they explained to me that my husband put in for a job as a firefighter and they were investigators and asked if I could I tell them anything about my ex-husband? During this interview, I was completely honest. They wanted to know everything I could tell them about his past. I told them everything I knew. That he had another child besides the kids that were living with us, and when the baby was two years old, the Department of Human Services found the baby in the tub with second and third-degree burns. The last incident I explained was how when the baby made too much noise, with the crib jumping and all the shrieking, he broke either one or both of the baby's legs, just for being happy.

They left after all that, and the investigation was over. Of course, he didn't get the job. A little while later, I was reading the paper and read that a child with my ex-husband's last name died in a fire. I asked him if he knew the child. He said that it was indeed his child. The child was in a foster home, and there was a young lady that got mad after someone slapped her. She waited for everyone to go to sleep, and in the middle of the night, she poured gasoline all through the house. Most of the people were burned beyond recognition. He called to find out about the situation, and was told he had to go to the morgue to identify the body. Of course, he hadn't seen his child since he was two years old. He couldn't tell if it was him, since he was burned beyond recognition.

Only one or two people survived.

He signed what papers had to be signed. There was no other family at the funeral. It was mostly teachers, the principal, and social workers. They spoke so highly of the child. It was a closed casket service, of course. I was with him throughout the entire process. After the services, a lawsuit took place. Since my ex-husband lost his parental rights, he wasn't entitled to the suit. It was supposed to go to the siblings. He had to fight to get his parental rights back, and it took years. He finally won. The suit was over $400K. He did nothing with the money besides sending his lady friends to different islands. His kids needed coats and clothes, and he wouldn't even buy anything for them.

Sometime later, one of my girlfriends needed a place to stay with her four kids because she also had just gotten out of an abusive relationship. My ex-husband and I talked about it and agreed that it would be okay if she stayed there with her kids until she got on her feet. I was in school for CNA training. One night, my ex-husband agreed to watch our baby in the evening until I got out of school and could pick the baby up. We had an understanding of our relationship, and even though we were no longer together, we can still have friends.

This one particular evening, a male friend of mine picked me up from school to give me a ride to pick up the baby from my ex-husband's house, and would then drop me off at my mom's house. When we get to my husband's house, I told the guy to park around the corner because my ex was crazy. I didn't know what he would do, even though we had an agreement. I left my pocketbook in the car and walked around the corner to my husband's house. I wasn't planning on staying long and was getting the baby ready to take home. Once we were ready, my husband offered to walk me to the train. I declined and told him I would call him once I got home. He insisted, and we went back and forth. Finally, he said he was going outside. He said, "Don't let me find someone out there waiting for you in a car, or your ass is mine."

He came back a few minutes later with my pocketbook in his hand. He had found it sitting in the passenger seat. All I could do was scream. My girlfriend grabbed her kids and ran upstairs. I had on a loose fitting short set and he came in the house fussing and upset. Before I knew it, it felt like he ran his entire hand inside my vagina. I felt something gushing out, but I didn't look. I just ran around screaming and hollering, holding myself. I ran upstairs to where my girlfriend was with her children. She looked at me and said, "Oh my god,

Silent Tears I've Cried by Shelly Knox

he cut you down there. You're bleeding!"

When I looked down, blood was everywhere. I was never in so much pain. I ran downstairs to look for him, but I didn't see him. I turned over the China cabinet and whatever else I could mess up. I called the police. When they came, all they told me was to go home and take a shower and that I would feel better the next day after we both slept if off. The pain was just as bad the next day. I went to the sex crimes unit at that police station and filed my report. He didn't go to jail, but it was on his record.

From that day to this one, I still haven't seen my friend that dropped me off.

Chapter 25
Understanding

People don't understand the way things work. An infant, a young girl, or a teenager. They can't talk to you, not really. They don't know how to tell someone if someone is hurting them. And when they tell you as best as they can, you have to do what you must do to protect your child. There is no way a child can fight against big, grown men.

Of course, this was me. I had no way to win. What was pain to me was pleasure to those men. There's no way I could've been normal after the trauma and abuse I endured. That's something that sticks with you for life. They say you must forgive, and in my family, they say to just move on and forget. I disagree. It's hard to forget because it was very painful, and I try within my heart to be forgiven. They had no idea why I always cried as a baby. It started as an infant and it went on and on throughout my childhood.

People make judgements because they look at you, not knowing you feel dirty, and you're depressed to the point of becoming suicidal. They didn't know how I would cry all the time. I never knew how to carry myself. I never had a childhood. When going through this type of trauma, these are symptoms a person might have. Prayer, counseling, and reading the Bible have helped me through. I was in the dark, and God was with me every step of the way. When I began to know the words of prayer, I prayed and prayed for things to come to an end.

Chapter 26
Health Issues

I was always overweight as a child. At the age of 10, I was bullied terribly at school. This one particular time, there was a one-on-one fight at school. I fell and hit my head pretty hard. This one particular girl felt as though she had to bully me every day. She pushed me and I fell back and hit my head.

My mom came to the school and complained the next day after my mom left. The girl came to me and apologized; I went to sit down; I hollered and started seizing ever since.

I had my first gastric bypass done at 18yrs old, and the stress from the surgery led to me having seizures again. When I had the gastric bypass, my family automatically assumed I was on drugs or had AIDS. Fifteen years later, I had gained the weight back and was planning to have the surgery done again.

I got cleared to have the surgery and insurance

was clear, too. The doctor started the procedure, but come to find out, I needed to have another procedure done before the surgery. I had obstruction of the small and large intestines. Basically, it was full of poop. The doctor said he didn't know how I could work a regular job and have no pain. He said in all his years of practice; he had never seen a case like mine with the person having no pain at all. He said if I had gone another week like that, I would have died.

So, with him not being able to get a clearance on the spot from insurance, I got two surgeries for the price of one, since it was a matter of life or death. Then, I had an infection in my incision. I had to be readmitted to the hospital, and the doctor had to cut my incision open again to drain it. He sent me home with instructions on how to care for it until it closed, which would be about six months. A nurse came to my house two to three times a week. The smell from the incision was terrible, like old, rotten meat. The cut was from the top to the bottom of my stomach. Of course, by my healing with keloids, I could never wear a two-piece bathing suit. I was losing weight, though. I wasn't home long before I had to be rushed back to the hospital because I couldn't breathe. Come to find out I had a DVT blood clot in my left leg that had traveled to both my lungs. (Bilateral/PE). I didn't know how severe the situation was. Two or three days after, they told me they had been really scared, because the clot could've travelled to my brain and killed me. They were grateful to see me okay, sitting there doing my crossword puzzles.

Flashbacks

For years, I had nightmares, and sometimes I'd get flashbacks of the trauma in my past. I cried in my sleep, not realizing it was only a dream. I visualized the things I had been through in my past, especially when I saw my cousin. He and other family members always called me names and treated me horribly, acting as if I didn't belong. All I could do after every family reunion or funeral was just go home and cry and have terrible anxiety and panic attacks.

My cousin passed, and on the day of her funeral, I had to work, but I could go to the viewing. My niece saw me getting in my car and she called me. I asked her where she was and she told me she was right behind me, in the car with other family members. The kids and I went to see her and the other family, but I had no idea my cousin would be there. Seeing him then, around the other family, was awkward because I knew he was going to say something negative, like he always did. On this particular day, he didn't, but he had a little smirk on his face. I wasn't sure how to feel.

I dropped the kids off and went to work. My client had a doctor's appointment, and while we were sitting in the doctor's office, I was thinking about seeing him that morning, remembering how he had treated me all those times. I thought about the smirk on his face.

Then, I was thinking about all the family who said he didn't touch me. I was so upset; I had to call my husband. A panic attack started, and I couldn't stop crying. My client became very afraid and concerned. She began praying for me right there in the office. By the time her appointment was over, I was a little better, and I felt terrible. I couldn't stop apologizing.

I wanted it all to be over. I had no idea it would last forever.

I always wanted to fit in where I didn't belong and

was never welcomed. I made myself and others awkward; I never knew how to communicate with others. Not many people wanted me around, because I was never understood. I always cracked jokes to make others laugh. I never laughed about people or made fun of others. Jokes were my way of coping. Sometimes I wanted to be around people and sometimes I didn't. I was always annoying, but I just wanted to be loved.

Because of all the trauma I went through, it caused me to be mentally ill with depression. Just because you go through depression, it doesn't mean you're crazy. Sometimes voices would tell me to do different things, or I would visualize things from my past. I knew it wasn't right, and I needed help.

As I mentioned earlier, I often had family tell me, "It's over with, just forget it. It happened years ago." You can't tell that to someone who was abused as I was for so much of my childhood and life. Everyone's pain is different. If you've never been molested, you don't realize that it's difficult to "just get over it," and everyone is different. Some victims have been molested once and they're in an institution for years and may never come home. Some victims might have several incidents and

Silent Tears I've Cried by Shelly Knox

handle it well.

I tried to take massive overdoses more times than I care to admit. A few times I needed CPR, and had to get my stomach pumped. I just didn't have the desire to live anymore. I was always told when you leave here, you go to a better place where there is no more suffering and no more pain. God knows I was tired of being hurt.

Even though I went through what I went through with my family, I still love them. It has to be love from a distance, and it has taken me years to realize this. Not all of my family is the same, but they do stick together. I'm done chasing people that don't want to be bothered.

I cried today. I cried yesterday. I cried the nights I was sitting outside on my friend's steps with nowhere to go in the snow and rain, wondering what my next step was. I cried the days they forgot my birthday, and I had to remind them, which happened more than once.

I'm tired of crying. I've cried all my life.

Life is too short. No matter how I was treated by you, I'm still going to be me and love you. Always.

Chapter 27
New Beginning of the End

The Moment I Chose to Live

Eventually, things turned around. I met the first true love. A true gentleman, finally, that I'd ever truly known. I asked myself if it was real. We got married and everything has been wonderful. Perfect, even. Some of my in-laws treat me as my family did in the past, saying I am too dark and not attractive enough for him, but things with my husband are perfect. Just when I thought things would never get better, I met the perfect guy.

My Love, My Heart, My Everything

I never thought we'd come across each other.

When I met you, I chose to live.

My husband differed from any other man I've ever known. We had lived in the same neighborhood when we were little, and even started kindergarten at the same school, at the same time. We had the same teachers, the same principal, and the same friends, but we don't remember each other. We even visited the same friend's house (a brother and a sister). My husband came over to play the drums and I came over to do girly stuff. (I was molested by my girlfriend's older brother.) Still, we don't remember ever meeting each other.

How grateful I am to have someone who loves me just for me. He cares for me and enjoys being with me. He is not abusive. We're just perfect for each other. I didn't know the simplest things when I met him, like opening the car door for him after he had opened my door for me. We enjoy being with each other, and we're just happy together. He'll never understand what I've been through. I don't really understand it myself. But he accepts me with all my flaws.

Silent Tears I've Cried by Shelly Knox

He's my only loyal friend. He holds me and tells me he loves me, and lets me know everything is going to be okay. I get hugs, kisses, and smiles from him, and a prayer every morning before he goes to work. We laugh, joke, and we're truthful. We're like grade school sweethearts. He's the only person I've ever had in my life that was ever interested in praying with me. That's how I know God sent him to me. We're there for each other and can talk to each other about anything. He's never criticized me or been judgmental or abusive. The biggest fight he and I might have is what's for dinner on a weekend.

He lets me know how much he truly loves me. He knows that my love comes from the heart, and he wouldn't do anything to take that away from me.

He's like the missing piece to my puzzle. The beginning of the end!

Chapter 28
Working for a
Blessing

I received a phone call one Saturday morning. A friend that often referred me to clients asked if I was working, which I wasn't. She asked if I would be interested in helping this man take care of his wife. She told me it was about a 40-minute drive from my house and it would be for a few days a week. I said sure and got the number from her. When I called, there was no answer, but I left a message, saying I heard he needed help to care for his wife.

Mr. Goldsborough called me back.

I asked him if I could call him Mr. G. and he agreed. I told him I was available to help him with caring for his wife.

He was upset and told me he couldn't afford to hire me. How did you get my number?

I said, "Don't worry about that. What time can I start?"

He said, "Wait a minute. Is this some kind of joke or something? Nobody works for free."

"Consider it a blessing," I said.

He couldn't believe it. He said, "I know blessings happen, but this is unreal. I just can't believe it."

After a week of work, I was asked how things were working out with my client. I told my friend that I know he said he needed help with his wife, but he needed care for himself as well.

From the moment I walked into his home, he would talk nonstop until it was time for me to go home. I couldn't get a word in. He needed someone to talk to, so I listened.

I barely did anything for his wife. I would just sit with her while he went to the store. Mr. G would do total care most of the time and he was good at it, not to mention very particularly with the way he cared for her.

They both were clients like no other, and we became more like family. I had been praying to learn more about the Bible and hoping to find a church home. Mr. G was always talking about his church, and he was always reading the bible. One day, he asked if I would come to his church with him. I agreed, but it took a while for me to go. But now, I'm a member.

God sent me this elderly couple, the nicest people you could ever meet. They treated me so much like family. I cared about them so much.

A few months after working for Mr. G, I asked him what he did for his recent birthday. He said nobody ever called or came by and that he didn't do anything.

When he said that, I was determined that if I was still working for him the following year, I would do something for him.

Silent Tears I've Cried by Shelly Knox

He was the most generous man, always doing something for someone like donating to all the ministries that were in need of help. Mr. G truly always helped any and everybody he could.

The next time his birthday was approaching, I got together with some people in the church, and we started planning a SURPRISE birthday party for him. It was so much fun to plan. When he arrived, he still had no idea the party was for him, until he started looking around at everyone. He saw his cousins, and they were saying surprise. It was an awesome party; almost 80 people came. He was so happy. He said that he had no idea he was loved by so many.

He's like the brother, I never had, always joking around with me like family. One day I had a bag full of candy from the party. I don't normally eat candy. I was digging in the bag, and before I knew it, Mr. G grabbed the bag and I had to chase him downstairs to the basement for the candy. I still haven't found it, but what a funny thing.

We have truly become the best of friends.

We're all so grateful for each other.

To Mrs. Shirley: If you're alone, I will be your shadow. If you want to cry, I will be on your shoulder. If you need a hug, I will be your pillow. If you need to be happy, I will make you smile. But anytime you need a friend, I will just be me.

Silent Tears I've Cried by Shelly Knox

Serenity Prayer

God, grant me the serenity to accept the things I cannot change, the courage to change the things I can, and the wisdom to know the difference.

Silent Tears I've Cried by Shelly Knox

Acknowledgements

Foremost, I want to thank God. Without him, I wouldn't have made it through to tell my story.

Thank you to my husband, who supports me in every way. I can cry on his shoulder, talk to him, and if I need space, he gives me that, too.

My children & grandchildren. I didn't know or understand my role. I did my best.

Thank you to my mothers.

Thank You, Mr. V, my Latin Teacher. When I'd come to school and didn't know how to handle what I was going through, I thank you for being there to help me through. You continued to push me and gave me help and showed me what to do. I didn't know how to cope, and you helped. Your unconditional love and constant protective interventions enabled me to feel that maybe my life was worth living.

Mom Dit, thank you and your family for taking me in with no problem and always treating me as a family.

Author Diana Hill, thank you for helping me with everything pertaining to my book and referring me to different projects.

Donna Garey and Jean Moore, thank you ladies for just being there. I couldn't have done it without you and Mr. V., Mr. G, Sharmaine Mickens and Jose Dopwell. Thank you.

Special thanks to you, Mr. & Mrs. Goldsborough and Michelle Jefferson.

Daniel Serrano Jr. and Paul T. Knox, thank you for your help with the book.

I can't leave out the people who have hurt me throughout life. Without you, there would be no story to tell, and I wouldn't know how to help others.

I'm trying my best to learn to forgive others and I have to pray for them as well.

About the Author

She is a caring wife, a loving mother, grandmother, godmother, caretaker, a sister, cousin too many and a friend to all. She has a heart of gold and is a corny comedian who tries to hide her tears behind her smile. A Philadelphia native, educated in the public school system, and even though she didn't complete high school, she could still take a Nursing Assistant Course at a trade school, and years later in another state, she went to a college to retake the course for that state to keep her job as a CNA. She worked in several hospitals (different capacities) and had private duty as a Certified Nursing Assistant from the age of 18 to the present (home health care worker). Even though she could not finish high school due to the trauma she endured, she still managed to live and enjoy life.

She doesn't keep friends long, only her childhood friends who have been there for her since fifth grade. They know and understand her.

Her family is judgmental and hates her because of what she's been through. She was young she had no idea what was happening to her.

The love of her life is her husband, children, grandchildren, and can't forget about the Blue Crabs.

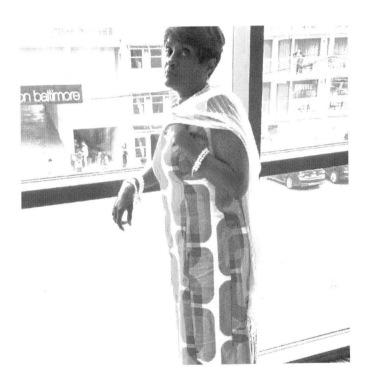

Silent Tears I've Cried by Shelly Knox

THE QUEEN BEHIND THE BLACK MASK

When you're told all your life, you're ugly every day, from the people that you were raised by and supposed to be loved by, that's what you eventually are going to believe. They raped me and stripped me of all my dignity. I was never told I was pretty. That's caused me to have low self- esteem, all my life. How do you know you're worthy; how do you know to love the skin you're in; when all you've been led to believe is that you're nothing.

Because of all the trauma in my life, I was always ashamed of how I looked. I became comfortable when covid 19 came, because than I had to wear a mask.

I became comfortable wearing the mask,

because my face was hidden.

I still wore mine when the mandate was lifted.

Black is my favorite color.

The black mask hid the scars, tears and fear that was hidden behind the years.

Now I hold my head high,

I walk with a purpose in a smile.

I might from time-to-time cry from the pain,

Because for me the pain will always be,

And it will be okay to cry.

My head is held high,

And I'll say thanks to Jesus,

Who's yet teaching me, how to love myself.

In order to love anyone, you must learn to love
yourself, first.

It wasn't easy! You must pray,

Have faith and believe. He'll see you through!

Silent Tears I've Cried by Shelly Knox

My Hobby

"This is my time to celebrate me. If
no one else will celebrate you, learn
to celebrate yourself."

~ Diana Hill, Author

Made in the USA
Middletown, DE
03 October 2023

39990328R00102